The Cr~~ystal~~ Workbook

Ali Maq Peregrine

www.capallbann.co.uk

The Crystal Workbook

ISBN 186163 319 X
ISBN 13 9781861633194

Cover design by HR Design - www.hr-design.co.uk
Cover and internal artwork by Ali Maq Peregrine

Published by:

Capall Bann Publishing
Auton Farm
Milverton
Somerset
TA4 1NE

This book is dedicated to Benny Vee and Serious who watched me type it, to my friends from EFC and before who were with me at the very beginning, and finally to my last-minute rescuer, who rescued me at the last minute. Everything unattempted is impossible.

Ali Maq Peregrine

Contents

Introduction

The Crystal Workbook is the culmination of 20 or so years of my ongoing interest in crystals, rocks, gemstones and minerals. I acquired my first tumbled stones as a child; many of these still live and work with me. Over the last decade I have been actively studying, learning; acquiring knowledge, experience, and I hope wisdom from working with the energies of crystals. I am a qualified Crystal Healing practitioner, and have a continuing interest in complementary therapies, Nature, ancient and modern spiritual practices, and in universal balance and peace.

This book will give you the relevant background information as well as helping you learn how to work with the energies of crystals, in an experiential, hands-on, practical way. There are exercises and meditations throughout the book, and you are invited to write up your own experiences in a journal that will not only become your own personal resource, but will help chart your progress, and I hope will encourage you further along the path of Crystal Healing.

The Crystal Workbook is divided into three main sections: Theory, Practice, and an Index of Crystal Properties. At the back of the book there is a list of References and Resources that contains details of other relevant information sources, as well as a selection of resources providing formal, certified, accredited and structured training in Crystal Healing (which there is no substitute for should you wish to start your own Crystal Healing practice).

1

How To Use The Crystal Workbook

There is no better place to begin than the beginning! If you are new to Crystal Healing, then I recommend you read the Theory section first, before working systematically through the Practice section from beginning to end, at your own pace. If you wish to expand and extend your existing knowledge and experience in Crystal Healing, please use this book as a reference for both practice and information, and dip into the appropriate sections as needed.

May the Stones bless you with inspiration, wisdom and healing!

Blessings
Ali Maq Peregrine

Part 1: Theory

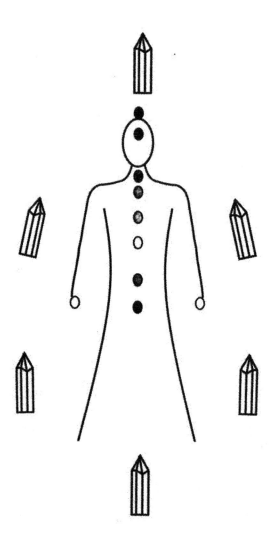

1. Definition and Origins of Crystals

What Is A Crystal?

A crystal is a mineral whose atomic structure is regular and forms a symmetrical crystalline lattice, repeating the same recognisable pattern or shape.

Crystals only form where conditions such as temperature and pressure are right, and will grow by constructing a molecular lattice, repeating the same regular inner shape over and over, until there are no more mineral salts and chemical compounds present in solution for that particular type of crystal to grow any larger, or until the temperature and pressure changes and conditions become less favourable for the crystal to grow.

Harder crystals, such as Diamond and Quartz, form at a higher temperature and under greater pressure than softer minerals such as Calcite and Fluorite.

There are seven different classifications of crystalline shape: Cubic (having a cube as the basic repeated molecular lattice shape – for example Pyrite), Trigonal (based on a triangle – examples are Quartz and Tourmaline) Hexagonal (based on a hexagon-shaped molecular lattice – for example Aquamarine), Orthorhombic (based on a rhombus or diamond shape – for example Topaz), Tetragonal (a rectangle – for example Apophyllite), Monoclinic (based on a parallelogram – examples are Azurite and Selenite), and Triclinic (based on a trapezium shape – for example Kyanite).

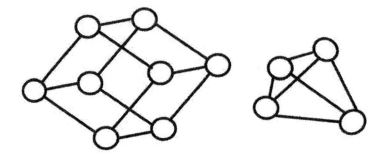

However, the inner lattice form is not always reflected in the outer form that the crystal takes – Tourmaline and Quartz are both based upon a Trigonal molecular lattice, which in Tourmaline is visually obvious, as it is a three-sided crystal with a triangular cross-section. In Quartz, the Trigonal molecular lattice results in a six-sided crystal with triangular faces at the termination. Conversely, there are certain minerals with no regular crystalline lattice shape that are also regarded as crystals, for example Amber and Moldavite. These are classified as Amorphous minerals.

The Origin of Crystals - A Potted History from The Big Bang To The Present

The Big Bang theory is currently the most popular of the Universe Inflationary Theories, all of which propose a chain of events that attempt to explain the origins and existence of the Universe. The scientist Edwin Hubble made the discovery in 1929 that the Universe is expanding, by observing that other galaxies are moving away from ours. This led to the Big Bang Theory (and the other Universe Inflationary Theories), which most people are aware of today.

The Big Bang Theory states that the very beginnings of everything originate with the appearance of a singularity amidst the nothingness. Space did not exist. A singularity is a zone of infinite density, intense gravitational pressure, incredibly small size and extremely high temperature. In almost no time, the singularity went from very, very small and hot to incredibly vast and very cool. This can be likened more to a balloon inflating than to an explosion. This expansion of the singularity gave rise to space and all of the matter in the Universe.

Attracted towards each other by the forces of gravity, particles of matter clumped together, the gravitational pressure causing them to heat up. These were the beginnings of stars, each one a protosun.

The life-force energies of the Mineral Kingdom on Earth originated with the birth of our Sun, and the birth of the Solar System that encircles it. The chemical elements Hydrogen and Helium, of which the Sun is comprised, fuse to make heavier elements, releasing phenomenal amounts of energy as heat and light during this reaction. At the birth of the Solar System, the fusion reactions continued, creating further chemical elements, which are the building blocks of all life.

As ripples of energy caused instabilities in the spin of the protosun, fragments of matter split off from the Solar Disc and were thrown outwards, away from the centre, creating trailing arms that continued to spin, circling the protosun. These arms of matter eventually broke away over hundreds of thousands of years, forming solar rings. Ripples of energy caused the matter in the solar rings to concentrate at certain places. These concentrations of matter attracted dust and small particles from space (which originated both from the birth of the Universe at the time of the Big Bang, and from the remains of previous solar systems).

As a greater mass has a greater gravitational influence, these fragments of Sun, dust and particles eventually formed planetisimals, or embryonic planets that continued to spin around the protosun, and under the forces of gravity, began to form into spheres.

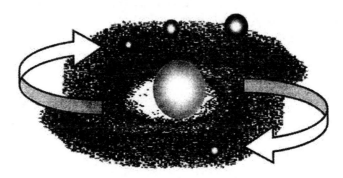

Protosun and Planetesimals

The heat from the protosun in our embryonic Solar System, and the gravitational pressure exerted upon the Earth planetisimal by its own mass caused it to become entirely molten. Centrifugal force, caused by the planetisimal's spin, drew the heavier elements, chiefly the metals Iron and Nickel, towards the centre of the new planet Earth, whilst the lighter elements remained nearest the surface. The gravitational pressure then caused the Iron and Nickel at the centre to solidify into a sphere, below the molten, fiery surface of the planet.

As the planet Earth cooled, the surface began to solidify and to form a crust. This crust was made mostly of the lighter chemical elements and compounds, such as silicates. At this time, many different minerals were formed, made up of diverse chemical compounds. This was the beginning of the Mineral Kingdom on Earth; similar processes occurred on the other planets in our Solar system, although the compositions of chemical elements differ.

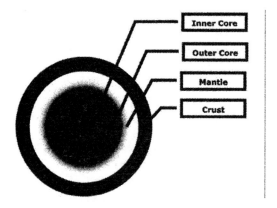

On the planet Earth, four distinct layers were formed: the Inner Core, which is solidified, due to the intense pressure at the centre of the Earth, and is made mostly of the metals Nickel and Iron; the Outer Core of molten Iron and Nickel; the Mantle, which is made of molten silicates and stony matter; and the Crust, which is solidified, and mostly made up of silicates and other stony matter.

Solutions, rich in elements and mineral salts crystallised over millennia, forming the primary or igneous minerals. As the Sun continued to provide heat and light to the Earth, weathering (erosion by wind or water) of these minerals took place, allowing the deposition of layers of small mineral particles to accumulate.

Under the increasing pressure caused by the weight of the many layers of mineral particles above, and over a period of millions of years, these layers changed, and became secondary or sedimentary rocks. The action of the liquid mantle beneath the Earth's crust, at the edges of the crustal or tectonic plates, caused the igneous or sedimentary minerals to be transformed by heat and pressure, into the tertiary or metamorphic minerals.

These processes for the creation and evolution of minerals are ongoing, driven by the Sun's constant heat, allowing the layers of the planet to remain in either solid (crust) or liquid (mantle) states. Some minerals are lost when they become molten, and other new minerals are made when the liquid magma of the mantle rises through the Earth's crust and solidifies.

The Mineral Kingdom provides both solidity and structure – the physical shape of planet Earth. It provides a stable foundation and basis for the existence of all other living things. There is nothing on the Earth that does not source its existence from our Mineral Kingdom - except meteorites, tektites and moon rocks captured by NASA!

Weathering of rocks and minerals by wind erosion creates smaller particles that form the basis for soils. Erosion of minerals by water creates mineral-rich solutions, which are taken up by plants and used for growth. Animal life-forms can then obtain necessary mineral nutrients from plants. Therefore the Mineral Kingdom supports the existence of all life on Earth.

2. Humankind and Crystals

Since the earliest days of humanity, certain rocks, crystals and gemstones have been highly regarded, both for their colour or clarity as well as for their inherent energetic qualities.

The earliest shamans and healers who were sensitive to the energies of the world around them would have been able to identify significant stones, and employ them in spiritual and healing practices. Often it would be the colour or physical attributes of a stone which gave clues as to its healing or spiritual properties. Over the ages these qualities have been further explored and refined, giving the wealth of information available today.

The ancient peoples built great temples of stone, aligned with the energies of the turning year or the patterns of the star constellations in the sky. These are to be found across the globe, for example at Stonehenge and the other stone circle sites in the UK and in France, and the pyramidal temples and cities in South America, such as Machu Pichu.

In ancient Britain, for example, it is recorded that the Druids used a "white stone", most likely some form of Quartz, in their healing and spiritual practices.

As human technology became more advanced, crystals and gemstones began to be carved and polished, in many cases revealing their inner beauty and colour. There are examples of ancient stone jewellery and spiritual tools in many museums;

as well as more controversial objects such as the Crystal Skulls, whose origin, age and purpose are subject to much debate.

The use of carved and polished stones in jewellery, whether for spiritual purposes or as decoration is as relevant today as in ancient times. Since the time of Edward the Confessor (1002 - 1066 C.E.) the Bishops of the Christian Church have worn a ring set with a polished Amethyst – to them a symbol of piety.

Throughout the ages, certain crystals such as diamond, sapphire and ruby, command very high prices due to their beauty and clarity when cut into faceted gemstones for setting into jewellery. Little regard is often given to the spiritual qualities of these stones, it is their size and visual appearance that attracts many people to them.

The use of polished stones in scrying, whether a crystal ball, or a mirror made from a flat, polished dark stone such as obsidian, is a spiritual practice that has survived since prehistory. The scholar and astrologer Dr. Dee (1527 – 1608 C.E.) had a "shew stone" – a sphere carved from beryl, for this purpose. It now resides in The British Museum, alongside many other spiritual tools, a great number of which contain polished stones.

With the reawakening of interest and the increase in popularity of many diverse forms of spirituality over the last century or so, there are now a vast quantity of resources available: books, courses and (more recently) internet sites containing information on all aspects of crystals and Crystal Healing. Crystals, rocks, minerals and gemstones are available to purchase in many shops, and at local and national events dedicated to all aspects of Mind, body and Spirit.

In furthering our spirituality, questions need to be asked about the ethics of purchasing crystals. Often the people mining the crystals do so for very little reward, working in unsafe conditions, especially in the Third World or war-torn countries such as Afghanistan.

Awareness of the origin of each crystal purchased, and pressure on the vendors and suppliers to guarantee fair working conditions and wages at the mines will more than likely push up the prices we the consumer pay for our crystals, but will help to end the exploitation of people who more often than not have very little choice in how they make a living.

Of course, it must also be questioned whether or not we should be mining for crystals and so scarring the Earth irrevocably; it is for each individual to make this choice, and to be responsible for it.

3. A Definition of Crystal Healing

Crystal Healing is a complementary therapy that utilises the vibrational energies of rocks, minerals, gemstones and crystals to restore harmony and equilibrium to the body, mind and spirit, so allowing self-healing to take place. All healing is really self healing, whether of the body, mind, emotions, soul or spirit, restoring harmony, vitality and balance and a sense of wellbeing.

How Crystal Healing Works

Crystal Healing works by using the placement of crystals on the energy centres of the body, and in specific symbolic patterns around the body and in the Aura to realign and rebalance the whole person's energy systems, to energise and disperse energy blockages, to relax, revitalise and to restore equilibrium.

The energy status of each part of the body and the locations of any imbalances are determined by the Crystal Healing practitioner via the use of pendulum dowsing techniques or by scanning the Aura a few inches above the body with their hands to sense any distinct differences in energy levels – these differences may feel hot or cold, "sticky" or "wrong".

The regular vibrations of crystals help to realign the whole person to their correct vibrational balance. Healing energy may also be directed and channelled by the Crystal Healing practitioner through a crystal and directed at particular areas needing more specific and focussed attention. The regular vibrational frequencies of each type of crystal make it suitable for certain types of healing; this is often also linked to its colour or form.

A Definition of Vibration

A vibration is a regular, repetitive movement at a specific wavelength (or frequency). Everything that exists, vibrates. Vibrations are caused by the movements of the atoms and molecules within a substance.

How Vibration Affects Everything

The interaction between all things takes place on a vibrational level. All of our senses (smell, touch, hearing, etc.) are vibrational. An example of this is our perception of a crystal's colour. It begins with the interaction between the crystal and white light (e.g. sunlight). Some frequencies of light will be absorbed by the crystal, while others will be reflected, or (if the crystal is translucent) will pass through it. The vibrational frequencies of light reflected or passing through the crystal are perceived by our eyes as the colour of the crystal.

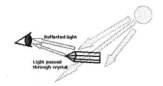

Crystal Healing has evolved over many thousands of years, passing on and developing a knowledge and wisdom first attained by our distant ancestors. It is both an ancient and a modern practice; its roots in the traditions, practices, customs, magic and wisdom of peoples who lived in much closer harmony with their natural surroundings, as well as being backed up to a certain extent by modern scientific knowledge. Over the last century, along with the great leaps forwards in science and conventional medicine, there has been a marked increase in the acceptance of the validity of complementary therapies and energy healing practices.

As complementary therapies have become more popular, the medical and scientific communities have taken a greater interest in them, in order to determine both if and how each therapy works. This is not a bad thing in itself, but in uncovering a scientific or medical truth behind what has been for centuries a sacred mystery, there is inevitably a sense of loss, a sadness that what was secret has been laid bare.

Also, both science and medicine seek to control and predict the effects of any treatment by standardising the dosage required, in order to effect a remedy for particular symptoms through analysis of the substances involved and testing under controlled conditions. As each human being is as individual and unique as each crystal, it is impossible therefore to generally prescribe certain stones in particular quantities or frequencies of treatment for any particular condition or ailment.

Often the root cause of an energy imbalance, for example work-related stress, is not reflected in the symptoms outwardly displayed, such as repeatedly suffering from colds. In these cases, Crystal Healing can here be effectively utilised to provide alleviation of the outward symptoms as well as to re-energise and restore overall equilibrium. As with all phenomena in Nature, Crystal Healing may not work in obvious or expected ways, as the systems of energy that make up a human being, a place or our planet Earth are both complex and interrelated.

4. Cycles of Coincidence and Correspondence

Throughout the known Universe, and across many cultures on the Earth spanning from the dawn of civilisation to the modern day, the number seven seems to resonate and have special significance. Seven has been seen to be an especially lucky number. There are seven colours of the rainbow, seven notes of the musical scale and seven days of the week. Seven planets were known to the ancients and used in both astrology and astronomy; there are seven major Chakras or energy centres in the human body, and there are also seven different systems of crystal lattice structure. The coincidence of this cannot be ignored.

As humanity progresses both scientifically and spiritually, more planets and more colours of light in the spectrum have been discovered. So, spiritually, more Chakras are becoming apparent, it is thought that eventually there will be twelve planets identified in our Solar System, twelve colours in the colour spectrum that we are able to perceive and twelve main Chakras, all corresponding to the twelve half-tones of the chromatic musical scale. Incidentally, returning to the first of each of these systems brings us to the supposedly unlucky number thirteen.

In fact thirteen is a number of completion – the thirteenth note of the chromatic musical scale bears the same name as the first and completes the scale, there are thirteen full Moons which make a year, thirteen witches make a traditional coven; and without thirteen at the table at the Last Supper as described in the Bible, would the events that followed have led to completion? (betrayal, death, resurrection and ascension – in other words, completion of a cycle of purpose).

Colour

Crystal Healing can take into account many different correspondences – the colour of a crystal, the particular astrological planet and/or star sign it is governed by, as well as its crystal molecular lattice shape, all may well correspond with its healing purposes.

Most people will have a favourite colour, several colours they frequently wear, and those they actively dislike. Colour affects every aspect of our lives, from traffic lights to food, from clothes to flowers, the world we inhabit is radiant with colour, and it can have a profound effect on our mood and our sense of wellbeing. Walls painted a certain colour convey a simple, yet effective message, for example, waiting rooms may be painted blue, to bring an atmosphere of peace and patience. Hospital wards are often painted a shade of pale green to induce calm and an atmosphere of cleanliness and healing. Red cars give the impression of being faster. Colour has crept into our emotional vocabulary too – ever had the blues, seen red, or been green with envy?

Colour correspondences

The following list gives a few of the more common colour correspondences. There are many in-depth resources available both in books and on the Internet that go into much more detail and give correspondences for many more colours and shades of a single colour. This is just a basic guide.

Red

Physical: warming, enhances physical activity, physically energising, activating, stimulating movement, life-force-energy, sexuality, sexual energy, strength, blood, birth, relieving overtiredness, survival.

Mental: motivation, instincts, willpower, boldness, dynamic personality, daring, extrovert, helps set and achieve goals.

Emotional: energising, balancing, passion, courage, creativity, enthusiasm, releases insecurity, relieves fear and anxiety.

Spiritual: protection, survival, grounding, rootedness, action, wildness, to make dreams reality, defence, creativity, connection with the heart core of the planet Earth, Fire/Blood connection.

Too much: danger, anger, too much of a good thing, fear, selfishness, aggression, lust, warlike tendencies, burning sensation, overheating, eruptions, stress, impulsiveness, impatience, boasting, abuse of the planet, rashness, rude comments.

Orange

Physical: warmth, energising, prevents clumsiness, improves appetite, fertility, vitality, attraction, relieves shock, practicality.

Mental: focus, encourages potential, adaptability, mental agility, positive thinking, organisation, direction, purpose, relieves boredom, allows instinctive thought, practicality, curiosity.

Emotional: creativity, artistic expression, playfulness, sense of fun, happiness, helps alleviate shock and trauma, is supportive, kindness, courage, sensitivity, banishes bleakness, eases transition through changes.

Spiritual: creativity, removes stagnation, brings abundance, exploration, prosperity, attraction.

Yellow

Physical: stimulates and balances the digestive, nervous and immune systems, helps body tissues repair, relieves allergies and intolerances, alleviates S.A.D and lethargy.

Mental: clear focus, decisiveness, resilience, tenacity, persuasion, imagination, heightens the intellect, releases mental blocks, relieves nervous exhaustion, improves communication, memory, awareness, improves concentration, banishes indecision.

Emotional: strengthening and cleansing, alleviates fear, improves self-confidence, releases jealousy, brings joy.

Spiritual: happiness, contentment, psychic ability, vision, visualisation, awareness, the Sun and solar energies.

Green

Physical: fertility, growth, rejuvenation, healing and health, beauty, releases sickness.

Mental: ideas, personal goals, accomplishment, optimism, sense of freedom, sharing, removes boundaries.

Emotional: balances emotions, allows expression of feelings and releasing of hurts, brings emotional growth, nurturing, disperses anger, releases jealousy, banishes discord, relieves feelings of constriction or restriction, improves relationships, dissipates dominance or subservience.

Spiritual: self-growth, removes boundaries and barriers to growth, allows change and growth, cleansing and balancing, empowerment, connection with Nature and natural forces, reaping what you sow, past life recall, prosperity, abundance, connection to Mother Earth / Earth Goddess energy.

Too much: jealousy, greed, envy, dominance, asserting power over.

Turquoise

Physical: increases energy, promotes health, strengthens the immune system, helps the body eliminate toxins.
Mental: individuality, innovation, increases interest in life, confidence.
Emotional: expression of wishes, emotional intelligence, improves the courage to be oneself, inner strength.
Spiritual: balances Karmas, for personal space and freedom, protection.

Blue

Physical: relieves headaches, cooling to inflammations, promotes the flowing of energy through the body, rest.
Mental: clear communication, the five senses, communication using all the senses, confidence, self-expression, releases blockages in communication, increases knowledge, patience, sincerity, reliability, ethics, listening and talking, interaction, detachment.
Emotional: uplifting, creativity, hope, friendship, relief from emotional turmoil, relieves disappointment.
Spiritual: protection, astral travel, tranquillity, inner harmony, peace, spirituality, opening to the spiritual and to Divinity, solitude, equilibrium, peace, devotion, distance, Water energy.

Indigo

Physical: relieves pain, gives sedation.
Mental: perception, understanding, intuition, profound deep thought, inward communication, inventive, philosophy, inspiration, clarity of awareness, problem-solving, understanding, focusing on ideas and beliefs, innovation, perception.
Emotional: relieves depression, releases emotional pain, need for personal space.
Spiritual: peace, connection, astral and spiritual protection and defences, connection with Divinity, inner peace, clairvoyance, clairsentience, clairaudience, psychic skills, solitude, retreat, Air energy, mystery, contemplation, deep peace.

Too much: can deepen existing depression.

Violet

Physical: rebalances extremes within the body's systems, improves coordination, speeds healing, calms hyperactivity yet energises lethargy.
Mental: inspiration, meditation – a quiet mind, clarity of thought, knowledge, deepens self-knowledge, independence, strengthens willpower, practical imagination, integration of new skills, relieves worry.
Emotional: empathy, sensitivity, heals sadness, relieves depression, brings balance and healing.
Spiritual: sense of service to others, peace, meditation, a door to the unseen, dreams, rebalancing, psychic perception, spiritual work, ceremony, ritual, removing obstacles.

Too much: daydreaming and fantasy, departure from reality, wishful thinking, fanaticism.

Pink

Physical: beauty, reduces the effects of disease.
Mental: self-confidence, assertiveness, integrity, honour.
Emotional: friendship, ability to love and be loved, marriage, romance, attraction, compassion, forgiveness of self and others, neutralises negativity, releases fear and anger, dissolves friction and aggression, alleviates feelings of complacency, improves sense of self worth, caring, tenderness.
Spiritual: harmony, self-acceptance, relaxation, protection, peace, attraction, love, beauty.

White

Physical: detoxification, birth, death.
Mental: clarity, truth, cleanliness, clear uncluttered thoughts, potential.
Emotional: peace, releasing emotional blockages.
Spiritual: purification, cleansing, enlightenment, psychic powers, spiritual strength, wholeness, completion, holiness, beginnings, the Moon and lunar energies, potential, reflecting light.

Too much: blankness.

Black

Physical: death, rest.
Mental: patience, truth, self-control, self-discipline, restraint, withdrawal.
Emotional: resilience, reclusiveness, withdrawal into the self, emotionlessness, grief.
Spiritual: grounding, purifying, revealing truth, revealing hidden aspects, surfacing imbalances, absorbs light, releasing negativity, imparts mystery, restfulness, manifestation, banishing negativity, for protection.

Too much: fear, emptiness, despair.

GRey

Mental: efficiency, cool thinking, clarity of thought, releases victim mentality.
Emotional: stability, neutrality.
Spiritual: restfulness, intuition into past lives.

Too much: depression, emptiness, boredom, draining, over-detachment.

Brown

Physical: stability.
Mental: transformation of thoughts and inspiration into practical reality, attention to detail, dependability.
Emotional: calmness.
Spiritual: neutrality, solidity, foundation from which growth can occur, desire to remain in the background, wholesomeness, naturalness.

Too much: dullness, stuck in a rut.

5. The Human Aura - Seven Subtle Energy Bodies

The human Aura is made up of layers of energy, collectively known as the Subtle Energy Bodies. They are arranged in concentric layers, and form an oval sheath surrounding the body. These layers extending outwards from the physical body can be thought of much like the layers of an onion, building one upon another to make up the rounded whole person, and protecting the fragile growing point in the centre. The Subtle Energy Bodies are connected and interconnected by further vibrational layers that exchange life-force energy between each layer to sustain them.

The Aura as a whole has two main functions. Firstly, it acts as a receiver and transmitter of light energy (known to various cultures as Chi, Ki, Mana, Prana, Nwyvre, etc.) from the light of the sun and moon, and from everything we come into contact with, such as food, the natural world around us, crystals, other beings, etc. and send it to the body's energy centres, the Chakras. The Aura connects us to all of the vibrations surrounding us, and to the energies of the mineral, plant and animal kingdoms, as well as to cosmic forces.

The second function of the Aura is as a protective layer. If disharmony of a physical, mental, emotional, or spiritual nature occurs, for example, if we come into contact with disharmonious vibrations, such as those from pollution, negative interactions with other beings, junk food, etc., the

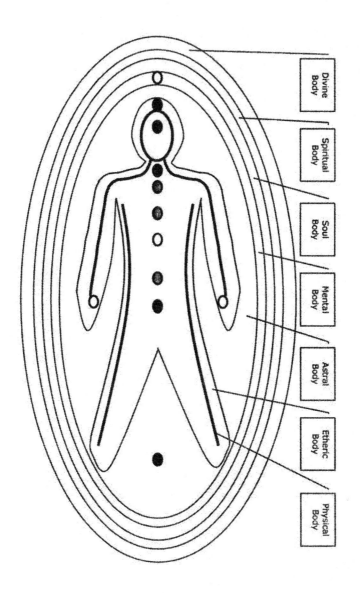

Divine
Body

Spiritual
Body

Soul
Body

Mental
Body

Astral
Body

Etheric
Body

Physical
Body

26

Aura can become de-energised and weakened, and holes may appear in it, allowing harmful energy through. These harmful emanations may cause mental or emotional imbalances, eventually manifesting in the Physical body as a physical illness.

The Subtle Energy bodies of the Lower Self

The Physical, Etheric, Astral and Mental Energy Bodies make up our Lower Self and form our personality. These are the aspects of self that are most apparent in our everyday life, and that others are able to recognise in us as individuals.

Physical Body

This is the densest of the Subtle Energy Bodies, the most visible and tangible of all the Energy bodies. Through the Physical Body, we are able to take in energy as food, and transform it into the energy needed to sustain all of our other Subtle Energy Bodies.

Etheric Body

The Etheric Body is an exact duplicate of the Physical Body, which vibrates at a higher rate. The Etheric Body forms the first energy layer of the cocoon of energy that makes up the Aura, and radiates outwards from the Physical Body, to approximately 10cm outwards. It can be perceived by sensitive individuals as appearing as a fine, greyish mist, somewhat similar to heat haze. The Etheric Body collects and transmits the sum total of energy from all of the other Subtle Energy Bodies. It does not have the ability to discriminate or distinguish between good and bad energy vibrations. Vibrational healing is mainly done at the Etheric Body level to cleanse and balance the energy in this Subtle Energy Body before it is transmitted to the Physical Body. Energy imbalances in the Etheric Body may eventually manifest as illnesses in the Physical Body if they are not addressed. Crystal Healing, for the most part, works through the Etheric Body, to disperse any blocked or negative energy, to restore balance and promote the flow of energy, and to treat any illness at its source.

Astral Body

The Astral Body is the next Subtle Energy body, and extends outwards from the Etheric Body. It is made up of the energies produced by all of our emotions. This energy is sourced directly from our soul, and when balanced and in harmony, manifests in us as joy, compassion and divine love. When the energy in the Astral Body is blocked or repressed, then negative emotions such as fear, greed, envy, jealousy, resentment and guilt are manifested. It is only when our emotions are blocked or repressed that these negative feelings arise and emerge.

Crystal Healing used at the level of the Astral body can help to draw out and dispel this repressed energy and open up the soul to receiving and giving joy, compassion and divine love. The colours in the Aura appear at this level and fluctuate as an expression of the emotions we are feeling at a given moment in time.

Mental Body

The Mental Body extends out from the Astral body and comprises the two layers of the Lower and the Higher Mental Bodies.

The Lower Mental Body comprises the energies relating to learned behaviour – the patterns of behaviour instilled during childhood, or due to the impact of traumatic or life-changing events, as well as the imprinted belief systems and ideas related to our culture. The Lower Mental Body contains the information on acceptable behaviours for our culture, the groups we belong to and the society we live in. This store of information enables us to function in this world on a day-to-day basis.

The Higher Mental Body relates to our abilities of logic and reason. The Higher Mental Body can help to link us to others; through this we have the ability to empathise, to give and express sympathy, and have an understanding of others.

The Subtle Energy Bodies Of The Higher Self

Soul Body

The Soul Body is the Subtle Energy Body that begins to connect with our Soul, the essential and eternal part of us that does not cease to exist after death. It is also known as the Causal Body, as it connects us with our Karma, through this lifetime, and those before and beyond.

Spiritual Body

The Spiritual Body is the Subtle Energy that is related to our intuition, inner knowledge, and the flashes of insight and inspiration we receive from out of nowhere. It is connected strongly to the Third Eye Chakra, through which this information is received. This Spiritual Body is representative of the area of high idealism and creative inspiration. As a part of who we are, it allows us a sense of service and working selflessly for the good of others. Connecting to our Spiritual Body enables us to acquire all these positive attributes, and to make a connection to our intuition and the inner knowledge of our Higher Self.

Divine Body

The Divine Body is the outermost Subtle Energy Body, made up of many layers connecting us to the Divine, however we each perceive Divinity. Initiates and Masters within any spiritual tradition have a greater consciousness of this Subtle Energy Body; awareness is much increased and enhanced by the spiritual awakening that occurs during initiation, or via an attunement to the Mastership level of a spiritual path. The Divine Body contains and emanates spiritual illumination, the truth and knowledge of who we essentially are.

Devas

Devas are the Subtle Energy Bodies of stones, plants and animals. They are more akin to our Higher Selves than the layers in our Lower Self Subtle Energy Bodies. We can connect with Devas via our Higher Selves, in this way, communion between the self and these manifestations of Nature can occur.

Sacreð Sites

Sacred sites have an energy emanation quite similar to that of the Devas. We can connect with the energies of a sacred site, and to the spirits of the place in a similar way as for Devas, through our Higher Self. In the same way we can connect with the energies of a particular place, such as our own home, and promote the manifestation of positive and healing energies there.

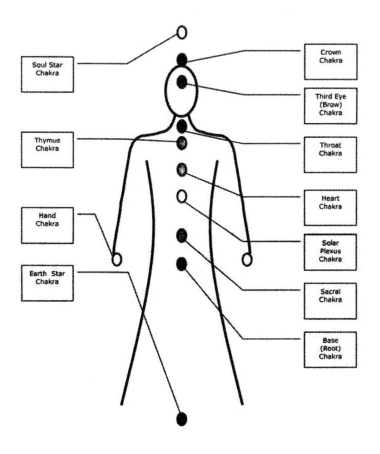

Soul Star
Chakra

Crown
Chakra

Third Eye
(Brow)
Chakra

Thymus
Chakra

Throat
Chakra

Heart
Chakra

Hand
Chakra

Solar
Plexus
Chakra

Earth Star
Chakra

Sacral
Chakra

Base
(Root)
Chakra

6. The Chakras

The word Chakra comes from the ancient Sanskrit word for wheel. The Chakras are the body's energy centres, often depicted as flowers with a various numbers of petals. They are vortices of bio-electromagnetic energy, constantly spinning outwards from the physical body and through the Aura connecting to all the layers of the Subtle Energy Bodies in the Aura. All the Chakras are also interconnected with each other.

There are seven Major Chakras, aligned and spaced along the spine. There are also many minor Chakras distributed at points throughout the body, for example in the centre of the hands. Each Chakra corresponds to a particular colour and is also associated with one of the ductless glands of the physical body. The Chakras absorb and distribute energy evenly, and so require a free flow of energy throughout the body in order to function properly.

In an unhealthy body, there may be build-ups of stagnant or negative energy, or there may be insufficient energy for the Chakras to perform their function. This may lead to physical illness, emotional or mental problems.

Major Chakra Correspondences

The following list gives brief details of the locations and the areas of the body governed by each of the Chakras. Brief details of the function of each Chakra and the symptoms of imbalance are also given.

Base or Root Chakra

Colour: Red.
Location: base of the spine, coccyx.
Governs: bones, muscles, lower extremities, sense of smell, gonads.
Properties: self-preservation, survival instinct, grounding, foundation, pride, health, prosperity, security, physical identity, dynamic presence, connection to the body and to the physical plane, Earth Energy, all issues of a physical nature, sense of belonging, confidence, roots, hackles, presence, trust, passion, lust, ambition, vigour, independence.
Too Much Energy: cunning, egotistical, aggressive, proud, over-ambitious, hyperactive, greedy, instability, rage, domineering, dishonesty, violence, highly strung, pushy, dogmatic.
Depleted Energy: isolation, fear, instability, lack of confidence, ungrounded, lack of ambition, insecurity, ill health, inability to accept responsibility, lack of resilience.

Sacral Chakra

Colour: Orange.
Location: below the navel or directly under the belly button.
Governs: spleen, kidneys, female reproductive organs, skin, adrenal glands, flow of bodily fluids, sense of taste, health, nourishment through food, emotions.
Properties: health, concern for others, intuition, balance, good humour, self-gratification, emotions, sexuality, desire, feeling, sensation, movement, discrimination, fluidity, grace, depth of feeling, connection to others through feeling, emotional identity, sexual fulfilment, sexual satisfaction, ability to accept change, Water energy, emotional issues, self respect, pleasure, creativity, nurturing, friendliness, ability to experience joy.

Too Much Energy: self-serving, petty, overly ambitious, explosive, aggressive, manipulative, selfish, lustful, overly proud, conceited, highly strung, power seeking, allergies, skin problems, kidney problems, anger, resentment, frustration.
Depleted Energy: frigid, shy, distrustful, overly sensitive, timid, hides emotions, overly fearful, emotionally hurt, guilt feelings, mistrustful of others, inhibitions, muscle cramps, anti-social, worrying, lack of energy, kidney problems, skin problems, allergies, fear, lack of interest in life.

Solar Plexus Chakra

Colour: Yellow.
Location: Solar Plexus area, a few inches above the navel.
Governs: autonomic nervous system, liver, pancreas, diaphragm, skin, digestive system, sense of sight.
Properties: self definition, personal power, ego identity, will, autonomy, metabolism, energy, effectiveness, spontaneity, non-dominating power, Fire energy, mental and will issues, self-worth, individuality, accomplishments, sensitivity, skill, outgoing, respect for self and others, cheerfulness, openness, expressive, intelligence, strong nerves, self confidence, flexibility, decisiveness, co-ordination and orientation.
Too Much Energy: very demanding, workaholic, judgmental, anger, rage, dogmatic behaviour, perfectionist, critical, mentally bullying, needs help to relax, stubborn, always planning but never manifesting, needing change, food intolerances and allergies, hostility, blaming others, obsessional behaviour.
Depleted Energy: depression, lack of self, blaming self, timidity, general fear, isolation, aloofness, feeling deprived of recognition, lacks confidence, hurt feelings, confused, poor digestion, fear of failure, apathy, poor judgement, afraid to learn, exhaustion, psychosomatic problems, muscle cramps, lack of power.

Heart Chakra

Colour: Green or Pink
Location: at the heart, the centre of the chest.
Governs: heart, lungs, blood pressure,
Properties: integration of opposites (mind-body, male-female, persona-shadow, ego-unity), love deeply, feel compassion, deep peace, centeredness, social identity, Air energy, love and spiritual issues, forgiveness, unconditional love, empathy, harmony, giving, humanitarian, adaptability, generosity, morality, gentleness, purity, innocence, seeing beauty in everything, in touch with feelings, desire to nurture self and others, healing, individual, trust.
Too Much Energy: overly critical, demanding, possessive, manic depression, angry, jealous, blaming others, miserly, stingy, overconfident, callous.
Depleted Energy: coldness, devoid of compassion, self pity, afraid of letting go, paranoia, uncertainty, indecisiveness, lack of self worth, possessive, unable to enforce will, needs reassurance, allows self to be walked on, victim mentality.

Thymus Chakra

Colour: Turquoise.
Location: directly above the Thymus Gland between the Heart and Throat Chakras.
Governs: Thymus Gland, immune system.
Properties: immune system on a spiritual level, protects the Aura, connectedness, spiritual love, peacefulness, good health, compassion, inner peace, social interaction, fresh ideas, purity of thought, Water energy.
Too Much Energy: self destructive, destructive, impure thoughts.
Depleted Energy: illness, unease, negative thoughts, unable to move through boundaries and limitations, confusion, turmoil.

36

Throat Chakra

Colour: Blue.
Location: base of throat.
Governs: metabolic rate, Thyroid and Parathyroid Glands.
Properties: self expression, communication, experience of words symbolically through vibration, language, creative identity, sound energy, connection through all forms of communication (writing, singing, etc.), creativity, acceptance of change, judgement, sincerity, truthfulness, Air, Fire and Ether energy, equilibrium.
Too Much Energy: talking too much, devious, arrogance, self-righteousness, violence.
Depleted Energy: addictions, timidity, inability to express or communicate, weak, unreliable, inconsistent, over-reaction, suppress feelings, lack of motivation.

Third Eye or Brow Chakra

Colour: Indigo.
Location: centre of the forehead, between and slightly above the eyes.
Governs: Pituitary Gland, governs the hormones of the other Endocrine Glands.
Properties: self-reflection, (light) seeing, physical and intuitive, psychic faculties, perception, see clearly, archetypal identity, Light energy, intuition, insight, knowing, broadens the mind, spirituality, dreams, inner visions, questions, clairvoyance, wisdom, spiritual love, connection, charisma, sight, smell and hearing, Ether energy, purification, calm mind.
Too Much Energy: egomaniac, dogmatic, authoritarian, manipulative, ungracious, belittling, proud, mean, impatient, obsessions.
Depleted Energy: undisciplined, afraid of success, cold, bitter, envious of others' talents, non-assertive, oversensitive, impatient, worried, phobias, inhibitions.

Crown Chakra

Colour: Violet or Purple.
Location: at the top of the head.
Governs: Pineal Gland, sympathetic nervous system.
Properties: self-knowledge, consciousness, consciousness as pure awareness, connection to timeless spaceless all-knowing, knowledge, enlightenment, wisdom, self-development, understanding, spiritual connection, bliss, universal identity, Thought energy, higher spiritual understanding, linking to the Higher self, connection to Deity, connection to the spiritual world, Ether energy.
Too Much Energy: headaches, migraine, mania, egomania, self-importance.
Depleted Energy: depression, shame, low self image, self-denial, need for sympathy, feeling misunderstood, cannot make decisions, catatonic, lack of memory, diminished concentration, despair, mental disorders, Seasonal Affective Disorder.

Some Other Chakra Correspondences

Earth Star Chakra

Colour: Brown, dark earthy colours.
Location: approximately 12 inches below the feet.
Properties: connection to Earth energies, grounding, daily life energy, cleansing energy, information.

Soul Star Chakra

Colour: Silver or silvery violet, like UV light.
Location: approximately 12 inches above the head.
Properties: past knowledge, Karmic memory, timelessness,

interconnectedness, Karma, portals in and through the time-space continuum.

Hanò Chakras

Colour: golden white, colourless, pink-gold or grey.
Location: in the centre of the palm of each hand.
Governs: sensitivity to and exchange of energy information.
Properties: transmit and receive information, transmit healing energy, receive energetic information from the universe, sense energy.

7. Polarity of the Human Body

The energy that makes up every part of our being from the whole person right down to a cellular level is not static. Currents of energy constantly flow through the body in a balanced and rhythmic way, circulating between two polar points: one carrying a negative electromagnetic charge at the top of the head, corresponding to North in the Northern Hemisphere, and the other carrying a positive charge at the feet, corresponding to South.

The pathways this energy current takes are called Meridians. These run perpendicular along the body and have been documented and worked with for health-improving purposes

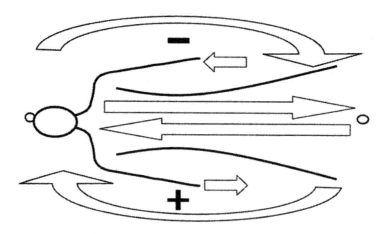

by different cultures since ancient times. Manipulation of the energy along these Meridians is also used in Acupuncture and Reflexology treatments.

The whole of one side of the body carries a negative electromagnetic charge, and the other side carries a positive charge. This varies from person to person.

The hand on the side of the body carrying the negative charge is better at receiving energy, so is referred to as the Receiving Hand, and the other hand is better suited to directing energy away from the body, and so termed the Sending Hand. Often, but not always, the hand that one writes with will be the Sending Hand.

Both hands may be used in sensing energy; the one that receives stronger sensations and is more sensitive to picking up disturbances and differences in energy patterns is called the Sensing Hand.

A Crystal Healing practitioner will scan their client's Aura a few inches above the body using this hand, to determine the location and the nature of any energy imbalances.

8. Crystal Energy Fields

Clear Quartz Crystal is ideal for use in healing as it can receive, amplify and emit energy. It has piezo-electric, electromagnetic and ultra-sonic energetic properties – it will emit electrical impulses under pressure, conducts electromagnetic energies and can both receive and transmit ultrasonic energy waves.

As a conduit of energy, Clear Quartz is most useful in healing, as the flow and magnitude of this energy can be directed by the healing practitioner.

Single-terminated Clear Quartz crystals are frequently used in Crystal Healing due to the predominantly one-way flow of energy, from the base to the tip of the crystal point. Energy may be directed towards the person to energise them, to a particular location on the body in need of specific energetic attention, or away from the person, directing any negative energy to be drawn off.

Double-terminated crystals have a point or termination at either end. These crystals have grown outwards from the centre, in opposite directions. This formation occurs where the crystal-forming mineral solution is held within a softer substance such as clay. Double-terminated crystals draw in, amplify, retain and emit energy at both ends simultaneously.

The energy field surrounding a crystal cluster is much magnified, due to the interacting energy fields of many crystal points. Crystal clusters are therefore ideal to use in charging smaller crystals; and may also be placed in the home and workplace to energise these areas.

Tumble-polished stones and spheres have a more diffuse energy field, emitting energy in a less focussed way, in all directions. These are most useful as stones to be held in the hand, or placed on the body during Crystal Healing.

Pyramids, whether natural or carved from a stone, have a distinct and focussed energy field, much larger than the stone itself. Pyramids are excellent for use in healing and meditation.

Part 2: Practice

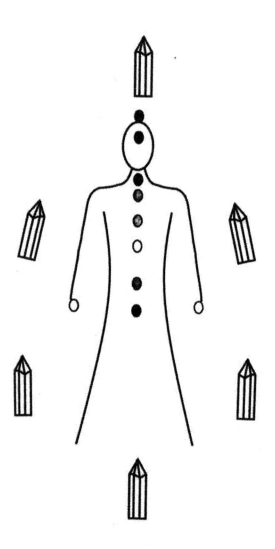

9. Basic Crystal Healing Kit

The stones needed for the exercises in the Practice section of this Manual and for use in a basic Crystal Healing session are as follows:

• Six Clear Quartz single-terminated crystal points, small to medium size, for use in layouts around and on the body.
• One Clear Quartz single-terminated crystal point, medium or large size, chosen specifically to become your working partner in Crystal Healing.
• One Clear Quartz single-terminated crystal point, medium size, very clear and sparkling. This will be used to stir and clear energy during the Crystal Healing session.
• One Black Tourmaline crystal, medium size, for use in grounding.
• One Smokey Quartz crystal point, medium size, to be placed below the feet during Crystal Healing.
• One Clear Quartz crystal point, medium size, to be placed above the head during Crystal Healing.
• One Pendulum, ideally made from Clear Quartz or Amethyst.

A selection of tumble-polished stones for placing on the Chakras:

• Two red or black stones for placing on the Base (root) Chakra, e.g. Red Jasper or Haematite.

- One orange stone for placing on the Sacral Chakra, e.g. Carnelian or Amber.
- One yellow or golden stone for placing on the Solar Plexus Chakra, e.g. Citrine or Tigereye.
- One green or pink stone or placing on the Heart Chakra, e.g. Green Aventurine, Malachite, Rhodonite or Rose Quartz.
- (Optional) One turquoise or aqua coloured stone for placing on the Thymus Chakra, e.g. Amazonite, Turquoise or Aquamarine.
- One blue stone for placing on the Throat Chakra, e.g. Blue Lace Agate or Blue Chalcedony.
- One dark blue or indigo stone for placing on the Third Eye (Brow) Chakra, e.g. Sodalite or Lapis Lazuli.
- One purple or violet stone for placing on the Crown Chakra, e.g. Amethyst or Fluorite.
- Two clear, white or pink stones for placing in the hands, e.g. Rose Quartz or Clear Quartz.

The choice of stones to use is an individual one; with experience, each person will have their own preferences within the broad spectrum of crystals whose colours or energies make them suitable for placing on each Chakra.

Basic Crystal Properties

- Amazonite – helps protect against the effects of pollution; soothing, calming and balancing; alleviates worry and stress; enhances communication and intuition.
- Amber – helps alleviate illness and disease; healing and energising; motivates and stimulates the intellect; protective, balancing and grounding.
- Amethyst – for relieving pain, especially headache; to sharpen the mind and the intellect; to defuse anger and stress; for energy balancing and protection.

- Aquamarine – to help reduce glandular swellings; to improve the intellect and awareness; for courage and shielding of the aura; for healing humanity.
- Black Tourmaline – for vitality and energy; to improve understanding and diminish fear; for protection, shielding and grounding.
- Blue Chalcedony – helps with mineral assimilation; soothing and peaceful; for benevolence and kindness to all; for protection during travel.
- Blue Lace Agate – soothing and beneficial; for peace and gentleness; to achieve inspiration; for attunement; for peace and happiness.
- Carnelian – to stimulate and to sharpen concentration; for increased energy and a love of life; for courage, inspiration and connectedness.
- Citrine – to increase energy and help improve the circulation; for confidence, clarity and creativity; to balance energies; to attract abundance.
- Clear Quartz – to energise, amplify energies and improve sensitivity and focus; to improve self-esteem; for protection, purification and awareness.
- Fluorite – helps to alleviate cold and 'flu symptoms; strengthens thoughts and soothes the emotions; to heighten intuition and ground spiritual energies.
- Green Aventurine – can speed healing; calms and clears the mind and emotions, increases decisiveness; for energy shielding; attracts abundance.
- Haematite – helps protect the blood and kidneys; improves willpower and decreases stress; attracts happiness; for grounding and protection.
- Lapis Lazuli – can alleviate pain and release negativity; amplifies thoughts and psychic awareness; protective.
- Malachite – useful in pain relief; amplifies love and loyalty, attracts success; transformative and protective.
- Red Jasper – nurturing and protective; helps the body eliminate toxins; for strength, focus and direction; to remember dreams.

- Rhodonite – helps in healing of wounds; instills calm, patience and balance; for meditation.
- Rose Quartz – nurtures the heart and attracts loving energies; improves empathy and trust; for love and self-love.
- Smokey Quartz – promotes equilibrium; eases worries and dispels anger; for grounding, protection and improved survival instincts.
- Sodalite – helps the immune system; improves logic; to still the mind; for fellowship and truth.
- Tigereye – can speed healing; for courage, optimism and to attract luck; to improve intuition.
- Turquoise – can strengthen the immune system; improves intuition and communication; protective, purifying and fortifying

10. Meditation, Visualisation and Affirmations

Meditation

Meditation is a useful spiritual practice for many different purposes and in different situations. The ability to still and calm oneself, to re-energise or re-focus before undertaking a particularly challenging task or facing a potentially stressful situation is a valuable personal skill. Regular meditation allows familiarisation with the movement and expansion of energies within and around the body, and increases sensitivity to the energies all around us.

In our modern, hectic, busy world there is rarely any time for pause, and we may at times experience a sense of disconnection from our essential self. Many people try to compensate for this lack by throwing themselves into their work, putting themselves under pressure to ascend the career ladder; to be successful. This can be to the detriment of other areas of their life. It can result in feelings of unhappiness, dissatisfaction with life, stress, and eventually lead to physical, mental and emotional exhaustion; a state of complete burn-out.

Meditation can allow for a reconnection with our essential self, for relaxation and refreshment, easing stress and re-energising, if only for a short while each day. This time, a gift given to the self, can have a positive effect on our overall physical, mental and emotional health.

51

It is advisable to meditate in a quiet and secluded safe space, although given sufficient practice, a meditative state can be achieved in almost any situation, however busy or noisy. Where a programme of planned meditations is to be undertaken, pendulum dowsing can be utilised to determine the correct time of day and frequency of meditations for a person at a given time and stage in their spiritual development.

During meditation, the body is usually still, either seated or laying down, and through a number of different simple techniques, the mind releases everyday thoughts and mental chatter, shutting down any unnecessary conscious thought patterns. There are many different ways to enter a meditative state: repeating a word or mantra aloud or inwardly until the sound becomes vibrations which set up a repeating pattern that allows the shift in consciousness necessary to enter a meditative state; becoming aware of breathing patterns; bringing the focus to each part of the body in turn from the feet to the head, and consciously tensing and relaxing that part; visualising becoming suffused with light or energy.

Depending on the focus of the meditation, the energy vortices of the Chakras may become larger and more potent as the Chakras themselves are opened, or the energy currents flowing around the body may increase in size or intensity.

After any meditation that involves opening the Chakras it is important to close the Chakras back down to a state often described as a flower bud with one petal open. This allows an everyday functional level of energy exchange to and from the Chakra without leaving it too open and therefore vulnerable to all sorts of energies, nor too closed and unable to assimilate and distribute energy.

Where energy of any kind has been accumulated, it is important to allow any excess energy to dissipate – this can be done by directing it back to its source with thanks, by directing it towards healing the planet, etc.

It is also important to allow time to regain everyday consciousness fully after meditation, to avoid feeling "spaced out" or disoriented.

Attempting to meditate when in the wrong frame of mind for it will lead to boredom with sitting or laying down still and quiet, and frustration at not having succeeded in reaching a meditative state. Meditating when tired will inevitably lead to falling asleep; however this is a lovely way to close down at the end of a day, and there are many meditation sequences that can be used to gently prepare the body and mind for sleep.

Exercise: Simple Meditation Sequences

Ensure you are warm and comfortable, either sitting in a supportive chair, or laying down on a mattress, the floor or other comfortable surface. Focus on your breathing, deepening and slowing each in-breath, and releasing stress and tension on each out-breath for a few minutes. Then go on to any of the following meditation sequences:

1: Visualise a beautiful, pure, sparkling white light being drawn upwards into the soles of the feet, and slowly progressing up the legs and torso a little further on each in-breath, energising each part, and filling it with radiant light, until the entire body is filled with light. This light is then either directed towards a particular purpose such as healing, relaxation or energising, or it may be directed to expand to surround the body in an oval cocoon of light. At the end of this meditation, the white light may be released to the Universe, it may be drawn within, to the centre of the self, or it may simply be allowed to dissipate.

2: Visualise a sparkling white light being drawn into the Chakras, beginning with the Crown Chakra, and progressing through each of the Chakras down the body, opening and energising each in turn. As each Chakra is opened, it may be visualised as a flower opening its petals. As the intensity of the white light filling the Chakras expands, it is allowed to move outwards to fill the whole being with light, radiating beyond the physical body as an oval, protective cocoon of light. At the end of this meditation, visualise each Chakra closing all but one of its petals, progressing upwards from the Base Chakra to the Crown Chakra.

3: A word, either an ordinary everyday word, such as "peace", or a sacred word or phrase from one of a number of Eastern cultures, such as "OM", is repeated, either aloud or inwardly, over and over, until the word itself becomes meaningless, and the regular repetitive vibrations of the sound allow the mind to empty of conscious thoughts and to enter a deep meditative state.

4: Perhaps one of the most difficult meditation techniques involves emptying the mind of all thoughts and images, and drifting into an empty mind-space. Any stray distracting thoughts that arise are dismissed, and the mind eventually becomes still and silent. The benefits of time spent in this stillness are immeasurable.

5: A meditative state may be achieved by gazing at an object, such as the reflective surface of a pool of water, a candle flame, or a crystal, and allowing the mind to become still. This can be difficult due to the eyes being open.

Visualisation

Visualisation is the ability to form and manipulate a mental image of something not externally visible. This may be an object not in sight, or a more intangible image such as the path taken by the movement of energy around the body.

The ability to visualise does become easier with practice. The following exercises may be used alone or in conjunction with a meditation, and are designed to build visualisation skills.

Exercise: Simple Visualisation Techniques

Ensure you are warm and comfortable, either sitting in a supportive chair, or laying down on a mattress, the floor or other comfortable surface. Focus on your breathing, deepening and slowing each in-breath and releasing stress and tension on each out-breath for a few minutes.

1: With your eyes closed, imagine that there is a blank screen before you, onto which any image may be projected. Visualise the image of an apple. Allow this image to form as slowly or quickly in your mind's eye as is comfortable. Take your time as you focus on making the image of the apple as detailed, accurate and three-dimensional as possible. Hold this image for a few moments before allowing it to dissipate. Repeat this visualisation several times over a week, or until you are confident that you can recall the image of an apple at will.

2: Allow the image of the apple to appear as before, but this time, when it is fully formed, turn it over and view it from all possible angles. Allow all of your other senses to come into play – what does it smell like or feel like. Visualise taking a bite of it and experiencing its taste. After manipulating this image in your mind's eye for as long as is comfortable, allow it to dissipate as before. Practice this visualisation until you are confident and competent.

3: With your eyes open, visualise the apple and go through both stages of the visualisation as before.

4: As part of a meditation, and once you are calm, relaxed and energised, visualise a stream of white light energy circling round your body in a clockwise direction, commencing above your head, and circling below your feet, before returning to your head area to complete the circle. Direct the energy to speed up and slow down. Once you are comfortable with this, change the path that the white light energy takes, determining which way it goes, directing it to form whichever patterns and shapes you choose.

Affirmations

Affirmations are a powerful method of encouraging improvements and positive changes to enter into our lives. To affirm anything is literally to make it fixed and firm. Thoughts, feelings and visualisations can become physical reality. Affirmations can be used to manifest a higher quality of life, and to transform negative patterns of behaviour and ways of thinking into positive ones.

Affirmations are usually written in the first person, and are intended to be spoken aloud to the self.

Affirmations should be written out before use to ensure that the wording is clear, entirely positive, and that the focus is on manifesting the desired result. An example would be the words "total health" rather than "freedom from illness". It is important that affirmations are realistically feasible to achieve, such as "I allow happiness and abundance to touch my life every day in every way"; and focus on manifesting independently of anything any other being may or may not have.

In order to maximise the positive effect, affirmations can be displayed where they will be seen every day. This reinforces the positive message and helps to overcome any negative self-beliefs, such as not deserving positive things, or not having achieved anything similar before. If an affirmation is accompanied by a strong and focussed visualisation, and is repeated often, it is more likely to become manifest.

Exercise: Write an affirmation to manifest more happiness in your life. Think clearly about the words you choose. Display your affirmation prominently somewhere you will see it every day, and when you see it, stop for a moment and say it aloud. Form a visualisation to help deepen your focus on this affirmation. Use this affirmation and visualisation for one week and write down any results you have.

11. Choosing Crystals

Personal preference must always be taken into account when choosing crystals. Some people prefer to work with rough, unpolished, natural stones, while others choose tumble-polished, carved, shaped or smoothed ones. There is little point in trying to work with the energies of a perfected, polished crystal if your heart is yearning for a natural, untouched, rough one. The cost of a stone also needs to be taken into consideration. Cut and polished diamonds, rubies and emeralds cost many times more than those in their rough, unpolished, natural state.

Natural, unprocessed stones and crystals have had less handling from the time they are collected from their natural location to the supplier where they may be purchased. The natural shape and form of a crystal will be, for the most part, many times more energetically potent than an artificially shaped, smoothed stone.

Some artificially shaped stones, however, have their energies enhanced by the shape – spheres and pyramids are two examples where this it true. A sphere emits a harmonious energy from every point on its surface, whereas a pyramid creates an energy field many times larger than itself. Both are potent tools for use in Crystal Healing.

Touch

Often, the crystal we need will feel more alive, instantly warm and pulsating with tangible energy vibrations. Where there are several crystals of the same type, with few visibly discernable differences, the hand can discern which one is the right choice. By choosing with the hand from among the crystals already in our collection, a stone to accompany us for the day can also be instinctively selected.

Sight

Sometimes, a crystal will draw our attention simply by the way it looks. Amongst others of the same type, one crystal may stand out in an indefinable way. Often this stone will be exactly the one we need, though it may not be one we have been seeking. In some cases, if uncertainty causes us to hesitate and not make the purchase, leaving the crystal that is calling out to us; should we return at a later date, we may well find the crystal still there and waiting for our return!

Dowsing

A pendulum can be used to select the right crystal from among several near-identical possibilities of the same type. Pendulum dowsing can also be used to choose a stone from a personal collection to carry with you for a particular time, event or purpose.

Need - by crystal properties

Researching the appropriate stones for a particular condition, unwanted feeling or situation is a good way to both ensure that the appropriate stone is obtained, and also to expand one's knowledge of the healing properties of stones and crystals. At the back of this book there is a simple listing of the properties of many commonly available stones and crystals. There are also an abundance of more in-depth resources available as books and on websites. A selection of these resources is listed in the References section at the back of this book.

Receiving crystals as a gift and giving crystals

As with all gifts, if you receive a crystal as a gift, it should be gratefully and humbly accepted, as the giver has put effort into choosing something with you and your interests in mind. The stone should be placed in a prominent position where it can emit both the energy of the giving of this gift, as well as the energies inherent in the stone. If the giver has little knowledge of crystals or of Crystal Healing, the stone should be cleansed, but not necessarily in the presence of the person who gave the gift, as this could cause offence.

When choosing a crystal for another person, it must always be kept in mind that the crystal needs to be compatible with them and appropriate to their needs. Any of the above methods of choosing crystals may be used, inwardly asking that the right stone for that person make itself known. Before giving a crystal as a gift, it should be cleansed and charged, and if appropriate, programmed for the appropriate purpose intended for the recipient, e.g. confidence, recovery from illness, etc.

Losing crystals

Sometimes, a crystal or stone may seem to disappear, or "wander off" from where it was last placed. Crystals may become lost for a number of reasons, including being genuinely misplaced, their whereabouts forgotten temporarily, or they may accidentally fall out of a pouch or pocket. Stones may leave us when their energies are no longer needed, or if they are not meant to be "ours" any longer. Many stones do indeed turn up again at a later date, when we are ready to receive their energies again. However, other stones may return to the Earth, possibly to be found by another person, quite unexpectedly.

Exercise 1: Choose (and purchase if necessary) three crystals or stones, using three of the methods detailed above. Record which crystals you chose, and your experiences of each method of choosing used.

Exercise 2: Choose (and purchase if necessary) a crystal or stone for a friend. Which method did you use? What stone did you choose and why? Cleanse and charge the crystal, and give it to your friend. What was their reaction? Record your feelings and experiences.

12. Cleansing (or Clearing) and Charging (or Energising) Crystals

Cleansing Crystals

All crystals will need to be cleansed and cleared of negative energy vibrations before use, as they can pick up and accumulate energies from everything they come into contact with. Whenever a crystal is handled or worked with, it will pick up energy imprints from the thoughts, emotions, and imbalances it comes into direct contact with. This vibrational energy is stored within the crystal and can then be passed on; by working with a crystal that has not been cleansed and cleared, any negative energy vibrations may be transferred.

Crystals in need of cleansing and clearing will have a decreased level of energy, or their energies may feel sticky. They may lose some of their innate sparkliness, perhaps becoming duller or somewhat cloudy.

There are many different methods of cleansing crystals; which one used will depend on the type of crystal. Some crystals are fragile, soft, brittle or water-soluble, so care will need to be taken, and a method of cleansing chosen that does not damage the crystal. Whatever the method used, it is the intention that the crystal will be cleansed that is most important. This can be stated aloud or inwardly when commencing cleansing a crystal.

Water

Crystals can be cleansed by immersion in a bowl of pure spring water for any duration between a few minutes to a whole moon cycle. Some people add sea salt to the water, but this has been found to be damaging to some crystals.

Where the bowl of water containing the crystals to be cleansed is placed in sunlight or moonlight, the crystals can be charged with these energies as well as cleansed, if that is in accordance with the original intention.

In emergencies, holding a crystal under a cold running tap, with the point downwards may be used to effect a quick cleanse. This is useful where no other method is immediately available.

Earth

Crystals can be cleansed by burying them in the Earth (or in a pot of Earth), for example in a garden. This will cleanse and recharge their energies. Any duration from overnight to a whole year may be selected as appropriate. It is important to remember whereabouts the crystals were buried, and also to realise that sometimes the Earth may not want to part with them!

Salt

Salt has, since ancient times, been considered a very pure and purifying substance. Crystals can be cleansed by completely covering them with salt (preferably a natural salt, such as sea salt). This method should not be used for soft, fragile or brittle crystals.

The crystals are left in the salt overnight, and any grains of salt that remain on them afterwards can be removed using a soft paintbrush.

Sound

The pure sound of a singing bowl, a bell or other resonant instrument can be used to cleanse crystals. The sound is played to the East, South, West, then North of the crystal, as well as above it and below it.

Breath

To cleanse crystals using the energies of the breath, focus initially on inhalation, breathing into yourself pure white light energy from the Universe. Then, on the out-breath, focus on breathing this light out onto and into the crystal, with the intention that it is cleansed. Repeat as many times as feels necessary for each individual crystal.

Energy

Crystals can be cleansed using any of the hands-on healing modalities and techniques (e.g. Reiki, Spiritual Healing, etc.). The practitioner connects to the energy source in their usual way, and then allows the energy to run through the crystal with the intention that it be cleansed. Crystals can also be charged in this way.

Incense Smoke

The smoke from incense has been used by many cultures to purify temples and people since antiquity. The natural resins, woods, and herbs, chosen for their properties of purification are as appropriate today as they ever were.

To cleanse a crystal using the smoke from smouldering incense, waft the smoke over it using a feather or your hand to direct the smoke, or hold the crystal in the upward-rising smoke above the incense. Sage, Sandalwood, Frankincense and Rosemary are good incenses for the purpose of cleansing and purifying.

Herbs

Some herbs, such as Sandalwood, Rosemary, Juniper, Cedar and Sage have purifying and cleansing properties. Crystals can be placed in a bowl and covered with fresh or dried herbs. This type of cleansing takes between one and three days, and can also be used at the time of the Full Moon, to add the charging effect of moonlight to both the herbs and the crystal. Afterwards, the herbs can be used in incense, or given back to the Earth with reverence.

Brown Rice

Crystals can be placed in a bowl and covered with UNCOOKED Brown Rice grains, and left overnight to be cleansed. Brown Rice reputedly absorbs negative energies. Afterwards the rice can be scattered on the Earth with thanks.

Crystals (clusters and grids)

A large, flattish cluster of crystals (such as quartz, amethyst or calcite) can be used to cleanse smaller individual crystals. First, the cluster needs to be cleansed, charged, dedicated and programmed to the purpose of cleansing and charging other crystals.

The crystal to be cleansed is then placed on the cluster, and left there for any duration from a day to a whole moon cycle, and positioned where it will receive sunlight or moonlight, or both.

This method of using crystals to cleanse other crystals can be worked in a different way, with a circle of individual crystal points encircling the crystal to be cleansed, or a large flat single crystal, upon which the crystal to be cleansed is placed.

Sacred Spaces

Crystals may be cleansed and cleared of negativity by bringing them to sacred places, such as stone circles, temples, shrines and holy wells.

With all of the above methods of cleansing crystals, it is possible to check whether each crystal is cleansed either by dowsing with a pendulum, or by holding the crystal in your Receiving hand, and allowing yourself to sense the crystal's energy intuitively. The energy of a cleansed crystal will feel clear, bright and positive.

Charging Crystals

After cleansing, crystals need to be charged or energised, to revitalise them and imbue them with an abundance of positive energy vibrations that they will retain until directed to release this energy. Crystals can be charged by particular types of energy to imbue them with the qualities of that energy, for example in moonlight or sunlight. Charged crystals feel more vibrant, sparkle with energy and will work to their highest potential. This store of energy can be accessed in various ways, such as meditating with a crystal that has been charged, by holding or laying-on of stones or by programming the crystal to release energy for a particular purpose.

There are many different methods of charging crystals; which one is used will depend on personal preference. Whatever the method used, the intention that the crystal will be charged is most important. This can be stated aloud or inwardly when beginning this process.

Water

Crystals can be charged by immersion in the pure water of a holy well, spring or the water of a sacred site. The energies inherent in the water and the flow of the water around the crystal effectively both cleanse and charge it. The duration may be from a few minutes to a few hours. The crystal will feel different, more alive when it is charged.

Earth

Crystals can be charged by burying them in the Earth (or in a pot of Earth) to reconnect and recharge their energies. Any duration from overnight to a whole year may be selected as appropriate. As the crystal is buried in the Earth, it is important to intend that it connects with the Earth's energy and becomes charged.

Sound

The vibrations of sound, from drumming, chanting, singing bowls, bells or other intentional sound can be used to charge crystals. The sound is played to the East, South, West, then North of the crystal, as well as above it and below it. Again, the intention that the crystal be charged is most important.

Energy

Crystals can be charged using any of the hands-on healing modalities and techniques (e.g. Reiki, Spiritual Healing, etc.). The practitioner connects to the energy source in their usual way, and then allows the energy to run through the crystal with the intention that it be charged.

Crystals (clusters and grids)

Crystals can be charged by placing them on a cleansed, charged, dedicated and programmed crystal cluster. The crystal will need to be left there for any duration from a day to a whole moon cycle, and positioned where sunlight or moonlight (or both) will shine on it.

A circle of individual crystal points may also be placed encircling the crystal to be charged, or a large flat single crystal can be used instead of a crystal cluster. Cleansing and charging crystals at the same time may be effectively done using other prepared crystals, providing that is what is intended.

Light (Sunlight and Moonlight)

The light of both the Sun and the Moon can be used to charge crystals. On a sunny day, leave the crystal in a location where it will be undisturbed (and not likely to cause a fire!) and in full sunlight all day. The light of the Full Moon is also most potent for charging crystals overnight, in much the same way.

Thunderstorms

The power of Nature's most unpredictable phenomenon can be used to charge crystals. Leave the crystal outdoors to absorb the energy of a storm. Ensure your own safety at all times during thunderstorms.

Sacred Spaces

Crystals may be energetically charged and revitalised by being within sacred places, such as stone circles, temples, shrines and holy wells.

With all of the above methods of charging crystals, it is possible to check whether each crystal is charged either by dowsing with a pendulum, or by holding the crystal in your Receiving hand, and allowing yourself to sense the crystal's energy intuitively. The energy of a charged crystal will feel vital, bursting with positive energy vibrations, clear and sparkling.

Exercise: Cleansing and Charging a Crystal

At a time when you will not be disturbed, and when you have one or more crystals that need to be cleansed (such as recent purchases or gifts), gather together the following items: a clean bowl, a bottle of spring water, and the crystals to be cleansed.

Fill a clean bowl with spring water and place it in a location that feels right to you – this may be outside in the garden on a sunny day, or a windowsill that gets a lot of light, or a special place set aside for spiritual work, such as a shrine or altar.

Place the crystals in the water, and look at them intently. Visualise the water cleansing the crystals, and the sunlight and / or moonlight charging them with energy.

You may like to say these or similar words: "Let these crystals be cleansed in this pure water. Let all negativity be washed from them. Let these crystals be charged in the energies of sunlight and moonlight". Focus on the words if you say them, maintaining the focus for as long as feels right. Leave the bowl in place for as long as necessary (you can always dowse with a pendulum to determine whether the crystals are fully cleansed and charged).

Give the water back to the Earth afterwards, with the intention that the negative energies washed out of the crystals are returned to the Earth, and that the Earth's own energy transforms them to positive energies.

Write down what you did and how you felt before, during and after this exercise.

Do you feel any difference in the energies of cleansed and uncleansed crystals? Describe any sensations, thoughts or feelings you experience.

Do you feel any difference in the energies of charged and non-charged crystals? Describe any sensations, thoughts or feelings you experience.

Did you feel comfortable using this method of cleansing and charging crystals, or would you prefer to use different methods?

Try two of the other ways of cleansing and charging crystals, and answer the above questions for the methods you chose.

13. Energy

To function properly, one needs to be both grounded and connected to the higher energies, allowing energy to flow through the body, between both Earth and Sky. It is important to also be centered and self-contained, so that any energy work can be done from a position of balance, inner poise and preparedness. It is advisable that before and after any spiritual or healing work, you ground and centre your energies.

Grounding

One of the first and most useful steps in many spiritual practices is learning how to effectively ground one's energies.

Grounding brings one back in touch with the energies of the Earth, the Universe, and the realities of the physical world. It involves establishing a strong connection with the Earth energies, bringing a sense of stability, security, solidity, and the ability to be fully present in the physical body. Grounding is a way of honouring our physical existence and our own body. A person in need of grounding would be prone to daydreaming, a lack of focus, vagueness, susceptible to influence by external energies and would be out of touch with the realities of the physical world.

Grounding can be achieved by meditation and visualisations such as growing roots like a tree or being magnetically pulled towards the core of the Earth, physical connection with the Earth such as exercise or gardening, by eating, or by using the energies of certain crystals to facilitate this. The energies of the Earth may be drawn upwards into the body from the feet, and the Sky or Universal energies may be drawn downwards from the head, mixing within the body and allowing connection to both Earth and Sky. Crystals and stones used for grounding are usually dark in colour, such as Obsidian, Black Tourmaline, and Haematite. Holding one of these stones in your hand, wearing it in jewellery, or meditating with it can gently ground your energies.

Meditation: Grounding

Sit quietly and for a few minutes in a place where you will not be disturbed. Have both feet planted firmly on the floor. Close your eyes and imagine that there are roots growing from the soles of your feet, into the Earth, anchoring you, supporting you. Visualise the strength and stability of this connection with the Earth. Feel the Earth's energies rising up and nourishing and energising you. When you feel grounded and firmly connected to the Earth, open your eyes. Record your experiences.

Exercise: Grounding With a Crystal

You will need one cleansed and charged crystal or tumbled stone of any of the following types: Black Tourmaline, Haematite, Obsidian, Lodestone, Smokey Quartz, Red Jasper, or any other Black, Brown or red stone.

Sit quietly and for a few minutes in a place where you will not be disturbed. Have both feet planted firmly on the floor. Hold the stone in your hand, and close your eyes. Allow the energies of the stone to gently ground you. When you are ready, open your eyes. Record your experiences. Do you prefer using a crystal for grounding, or the meditation?

Exercise: Grounding Meditation With A Crystal

Carry out the above meditation, this time holding the stone. Again, record your experiences. Which method is most appropriate for you?

Centering

Centering is restoring the inner balance within the body, being self-contained and being in control of your everyday energies. It is achieving physical, mental and emotional balance within the self and being aware of your own energies.

The centre of the body may be the physical centre of gravity, located just below the navel, or it may be located at the Heart, Solar Plexus or Sacral Chakra, or part way in between two Chakras. Everybody has a different centre.

Exercise: Centering

After grounding using one of the methods detailed above, focus on bringing your awareness to the very centre of your body. Breathe slowly and deeply, and allow yourself time to find your centre. If you used a crystal for grounding, bring it to the centre of your body, and hold it between both hands, allowing its energies to focus on the centre of your being. When you feel completely aware of your centre, energised and balanced, open your eyes. Record your experiences.

14. Connecting With Crystals

Getting to know your crystals

It is important to develop a connection with each crystal you intend to work with. This will allow you to ascertain whether the crystal is suited to a particular task or way of working, and if it is willing to work in this way as well as working with you. Some crystals can be very definite about how they want to work, and connecting with them will allow this information to be intuitively discovered. When you connect to a crystal, your Higher Self is communicating and connecting with the Deva (or Higher Self) of the crystal.

Meditation: The Crystal Cavern

Ensure that you are sitting comfortably, with both feet on the floor and one hand loosely on each thigh. Gently close your eyes, and allow your breathing to become slower and deeper, as you feel yourself starting to relax.

Imagine that you are seated in a cavern, deep within the Earth. It is warm and safe and comfortable. Below your feet, you feel the magnetic pulse of the Earth's heartbeat, soothing you and relaxing you with its steady, gentle rhythm.

As you relax, you become completely in tune with the rhythm of the Earth, your heartbeat becoming one with the Earthbeat.

On the walls of the cavern, arching around you and above your head, are millions of small, sparkling crystals, reflecting bright shards of rainbows and light all around you. Feel yourself bathed in this sparkling light, filling your entire being. You feel refreshed, and energised, and filled with a warm glow of happiness.

In the centre of the cavern is a small stone bowl, filled to the brim with pure, clear water. Within the bowl are crystals, cleansed by the water, and waiting for the time when you will choose them and work with them.

As you now allow the cavern to fade gently away into your memory, and you prepare to come back into the waking world, take three slow, deep breaths, and open your eyes.

Exercise: Connecting With Crystal Energy

You will need a cleansed and charged quartz crystal.

Choose a time when you will not be disturbed, in a quiet and safe place, and stand or sit comfortably.

Hold the crystal in your Receiving (receptive or passive) hand. Breathe slowly and deeply for a few minutes while you become aware of the energy vibrations emanating from the crystal. Consciously allow yourself to connect to this energy; focus on it and feel it travelling from the crystal in your hand, up your arm and into your torso. Take your time with this as the energy builds, and continue breathing slowly and deeply as the energy from the crystal fills your whole being.

Raise the crystal to your Heart Chakra and visualise your energy connecting with the crystal from the heart. Inwardly let the crystal know your intention to work with it for a particular purpose (e.g. protection, healing or pain relief) and state that this work will be in peace, love, harmony and for the highest good of all. Inwardly ask if the crystal is willing and happy to work with you.

Wait for the crystal to respond – there may be an increase in energy flow; it may become hot or cold; you may be aware of colours, smells or sounds; or there may be no discernable response at all. You will intuitively know what the crystal's response means, and whether it is willing to work with you in the way you intended. Trust in your intuition.

Inwardly thank the crystal for sharing its energy and this connection with you, then slowly lower your hand.

If the response you received from the crystal was a clear "Yes", you have now forged a strong spiritual connection with the crystal, you and the crystal are now in tune with each other, and can begin to work together for an agreed purpose. In this case, you may proceed with dedicating and programming (or enchanting) it to the purpose agreed upon.

However, if you received a "No", the crystal is letting you know that either it is not willing to work with you at this time, that it is better suited to a different purpose, or that it is meant to be with someone else. You may wish to meditate with this crystal, in order to find the answers to this.

Write up your experience of this exercise, in as much detail as you wish.

How did you feel before, during and after this exercise?

15. Energy sensing

Dowsing with a pendulum

Using a pendulum is one of the simplest and most visible ways of dowsing or sensing energy. Clear Quartz or Amethyst are both ideal stones for the pendulum to be made of as their energies are very easy to work with, although a pendulum made of any other stone or substance can be used, depending on personal preference.

Most people are able to pendulum dowse to some degree; with practice this can be a very useful tool in the location and dispersal of negative or blocked energy.

The motion of the pendulum will tend to be either in circles of either direction, straight lines back and forth, or a complete lack of movement.

Hold the pendulum chain or cord between the index finger and thumb of the hand you write with, allowing the pendulum to swing freely on a comfortable length of the chain or cord. Relax the muscles of your arm and hand enough that they can move freely.

Ask the pendulum to indicate the motion for a "yes" or positive answer. It will move, either in a circle, or from side to side. Then ask it to show you a "no" or negative answer. This should be a different movement. It is also possible to ask the pendulum to indicate an uncertainty with a different movement, although this is not necessary. These movements will be individual to you; there are no right or wrong responses, as long as there is a clear and distinct difference between yes and no answers. It is a good idea to check the yes/no responses of the pendulum each time before working with it.

To use the pendulum to ascertain whether a crystal is charged, hold it directly above the crystal and inwardly ask it if the crystal is fully charged. Wait for the pendulum to begin moving to indicate its answer. To detect negative energy within the body, hold the pendulum just above the body, and ask it to indicate any energies out of alignment with the normal energy pattern. Move slowly and smoothly over the body in a methodical pattern, either on one side from feet to head and back down the other side, or working systematically up the body on both sides simultaneously. Any energy anomalies will be shown by a change, increase or decrease in the movement of the pendulum. Further dowsing on these areas, using questions with yes/no answers will determine the exact location of each energy anomaly, and the nature of it. Asking a further question of "is this the truth?" is a beneficial safeguard against mistaking the information conveyed by the pendulum swing.

Pendulum dowsing may also be used to identify the location of something, by use of the "leading edge" method: holding the pendulum as before, physically induce it to swing back and forth in a line. Then ask it to show you the direction of whatever it is you have lost or are looking for. Allow the back and forth swing to oscillate in different directions, it will tend to swing furthest and most positively towards the direction of the item. Note this direction and take a few paces to the left or right and repeat. Then take a few steps forward and repeat again. The directions of all three lines, when extrapolated, should meet, giving the location of the item. This is called triangulation, and has many practical uses, from locating lost items, to determining the best place to live, and so on.

Sensing Energy With the Hands

The hands may be used in much the same way as a pendulum to scan for any energy imbalances in the body. Usually, one hand is more sensitive to energy than the other. Sensitivity to energy can be awakened in the hands quite abruptly by rubbing them together vigorously for a few moments and then holding them a small distance apart. In most cases an energy ball is felt between the hands, and with visualisation can be made to enlarge, to grow hotter or colder, or to be directed towards another person. Clapping the hands has much the same effect. With practice, however, only visualisation is needed to allow the sensitivity of the hands to awaken.

By holding the hands a few inches above the body and scanning through the body's energy field, any anomalies or imbalances can be detected. These will feel hot or cold, tingly or sticky, or may evoke thoughts, emotions or colours.

Exercise: Increasing Energy Sensitivity in the Hands

Practice awakening the energy sensitivity of the hands once a day for a week. Stretch, grow and change the energy ball between your hands in as many ways as you can think of – try it on as a hat, push and pull the energy, etc. Record any significant experiences.

Practice scanning your own energy field and note down what you experience. Scan the energies of stones, pets, places, etc. Record your experiences.

Sending and Receiving Hand

For most people, one hand is more dominant than the other one – it is the one used to write with, and the one that is better at tasks requiring dexterity. Usually this hand will be best adapted to sending energy, and the other hand will be more receptive and better at receiving energy. The following exercise will help to determine which hand is which.

Exercise: Sending and Receiving Hands

You will need two cleansed and charged single-terminated Clear Quartz crystal points.

Ensure that you are sitting comfortably and will not be disturbed.

Hold one crystal in each hand, with the point of the crystal in your left hand pointing inwards towards your wrist, and the point of the crystal in your right hand pointing outwards and away from you.

Breathe slowly and deeply as you sit for a while and become aware of any sensations in your hands or body – these may be heat, cold, tingling, pulsing, or like magnetism. Not everyone feels the energy in this way, some people even experience colours or emotions; we are all unique in how we perceive and respond to energy.

Now reverse the positions of the crystal points, and repeat the exercise, breathing slowly and deeply again as you become aware of any sensations.

The directions of the crystal points that produces the strongest sensations will determine which hand is your Receiving hand and which is your Sending hand - the hand with the crystal pointing outwards and away from you is the Dominant or Sending hand.

Meðítatíon: Senðíng Eneʀɡy Thʀouɡh A Cʀystal

You will need one cleansed and charged single-terminated Clear Quartz crystal point.

Ensure that you are sitting comfortably, with both feet on the floor and one hand on each thigh. Hold your crystal in your Sending hand with the point facing outwards and away from you, as energy will be focussed and sent outwards through the crystal during the following meditation.

Gently close your eyes, and allow your breathing to become slower and deeper, as you feel yourself starting to relax.

Imagine that you are in the cavern once more, deep within the heart of the Earth. You feel the magnetic pulse of the Earth's heartbeat, and begin to draw this energy into your body, beginning with your feet, and slowly rising up through your body a little further every time you breathe in. Feel the Earth energy rising through your body until it reaches your heart.

Become aware once more of the crystal-covered cavern walls, reflecting bright shards of rainbows and light. Begin to draw this energy into yourself, beginning with the very top of your head, and moving downwards through your body every time you breathe in, until it reaches your heart.

Feel the energies of the Earth and the energies of the sparkling light mixing in your heart, and expanding outwards through your whole body every time you breathe in, until you are overflowing with this energy It is within you and around you, filling the cavern with a beautiful glow.

Become aware of the stone bowl at the centre of the cavern, filled with radiant crystals and pure, clear water. Point your crystal at the bowl, and release the energies you have built up, through your crystal as a beam of light and into the bowl. See the glow that surrounds you expand to include the bowl. Become aware of the other beams of light flowing into the bowl, making the bright, beautiful glow all around the cavern bigger and brighter, sparkling and overflowing with rainbows and light.

Intend that this energy be used for Universal Peace.

When you feel ready, lower your crystal, and allow yourself to be filled up again with the energies of the Earth and the energies of the rainbows and light sparkling from the cavern walls.

Take three long, slow, deep breaths, and allow the cavern to fade, as you begin to become aware once more of the waking world.

Exercise: Instilling and Drawing Out Energy With a Crystal

To instill energy into an energy-depleted location using a single-terminated Clear Quartz crystal point as a conduit for energy, hold the crystal in your Sending Hand, with the point away from you. Allow yourself to fill with energy, and visualise this energy filling the crystal. Direct the energy out of the crystal point. Make clockwise circles with the crystal, decreasing the size of the circle as it approaches the energy-depleted area, until it finally touches it.

To draw out an accumulation of energy, hold a single-terminated Clear Quartz crystal point in your Sending Hand, with the point upwards, away from you and from the energy accumulation. Make small anti-clockwise circles, beginning quite near the energy accumulation, visualising the energy being drawn into the base of the crystal, then out of the crystal point and into the Universe to be cleansed and purified. Increase the size of the circles as the crystal is moved away from the location.

Alternately, energy can be drawn out using your self as a conduit and transmitter for this energy. This involves allowing the excess, negative or imbalanced energy to flow through your body, so it is best to approach this method with caution. However, it can allow you to glean insights into the causes of the imbalances or negative energy, and this information can be evaluated afterwards. Holding your Receiving Hand over the energy accumulation, and a quartz crystal point in your Sending Hand, held out to one side, with the point way from you, rotate the crystal anti-clockwise to lift the energy out, transmit it through yourself and out via the crystal into the Universe.

Exercise: Sending Energy

Practice sending energy through a crystal and moving the energy beam in patterns, either as the crystal is moved in spirals or waves, or with the crystal static and the energy patterns visualised for the energy beam flowing out from the crystal point. Record your experiences.

Note: After any spiritual working, it is a good idea to allow yourself time to re-balance your energies, and to become grounded. Dark, opaque crystals such as Black Tourmaline or Haematite are especially grounding, and may be held in your Receiving hand to gain the benefit of their earthy, grounding energies.

Sensing energy through a crystal (amplification)

It is possible to utilise the energies of crystals to amplify the energy messages received when scanning the body for imbalances. Holding a crystal or stone (spheres are particularly good for this work) in the Sensing Hand (the one which is most sensitive to energy), scan and note the location of any areas where the energy feels different, noting the sensations received. Further clarification as to the nature of any energy imbalances located may be sought via dowsing with a pendulum if necessary.

Energy Work

It is important to remember that during any energy work, where negative or stagnant energy is removed, an energy void or vacuum will remain, and if this is not appropriately dealt with, it will absorb energy from wherever it is available, including sources of negative energy. It is therefore vitally important to ensure that a balanced and positive energy is employed to fill this energy vacuum and to replace the impure, negative or stagnant energy that has been removed.

16. Dedicating Crystals

Before any crystal is used in meditation or healing work, it should be cleansed, then dedicated and blessed. Pendulum dowsing over a particular crystal can be used to ascertain whether it is suitable for use in healing or meditation, and whether it is willing to work in this way. Crystals should never be forced to work in a particular way or for a purpose demanded of them.

Dedicating a crystal will give it a framework of beneficent aspects to work within, allowing the crystal to be aware of what is being asked of it. Some purposes that crystals may be dedicated to are: love, peace, harmony or healing.

Dedicating a crystal is not the same as programming it, which will direct the energies of the crystal in a more focussed and specific way, for example to promote harmonious energies in the workplace, or to help with recovery from illness.

Crystals can be blessed at the same time as dedicating them. Blessing anything guides its energies towards only that which is beneficial and positive.

An example of a dedication and blessing for a crystal:

Sit quietly with a cleansed, charged quartz crystal in your sending hand. Focus on your breathing, taking long, slow, deep breaths for a few minutes to enter a relaxed state. Each time you inhale, visualise drawing into yourself a pure white light, gradually filling more and more of your being with its radiance. Once you are filled with light, allow yourself to consciously connect with the crystal, and focus some of this white light into the crystal, saying these words (or similar) aloud or inwardly:

"Stone of quartz, I dedicate you to peace, love and harmony. I bless you with the energy of pure white light for the highest good of all."

The crystal will now be ready for programming to a specific purpose.

Exercise: Dedicating and Blessing a Rose Quartz Stone

You will need one piece of cleansed and charged tumble polished Rose Quartz.

Following the instructions above, decide on the appropriate words to use, and then bless and dedicate the Rose Quartz stone. Do you feel any difference in the energy of the stone before and after dedication and blessing?

17. Programming (also called Enchanting) Crystals

Crystals used in healing work will need to be programmed in order to align and direct their energies towards this work. Stones used to create or enhance a particular atmosphere in a room, such as happiness or peaceful sleep are also programmed to emit their energies in this way. Programmed crystals will amplify the energy they absorb and reflect, and direct this energy towards the purpose they have been programmed for.

Crystals respond best to colours, images, sounds and thought patterns. Thoughts, feelings, visualisations and words have an energy that can be consciously transferred into a crystal. Crystals can also be suffused with healing energies, such as Reiki, and programmed to emit these energies over a stated period of time.

To programme a crystal effectively, first a clear visualisation or wording must be formed, and then transferred into the crystal as projected energy. Any visualisations should be maintained intently for a few minutes, and words should be repeated over and over, whether inwardly or aloud, much like a meditation mantra, until the crystal becomes imbued and in tune with this energy, and begins to emit it. Speaking, singing or chanting a programme aloud into a crystal is effectively enchanting it.

Some examples of words for crystal programming are:

Health and harmony
Balance
Protection
Peace and happiness
Manifesting abundance
Balancing the Chakras
Transforming negative energy into positive energy
Creativity
Healing when pain strikes
Calm tranquillity.

To Programme a Crystal

Firstly dowse over the crystal with a pendulum to ascertain whether the crystal is happy and willing to work within the programme you have in mind for it. It is important to never force a crystal to work in a way it is unwilling to.

Clearly formulate the programme in your mind; you may also like to write it down on a piece of paper that can be kept with the crystal. Be sure to include any colours, images and feelings. State the length of time that the programme is to be effective for, or at what time of the day it is to be active or passive (this is useful where a crystal is programmed for peaceful sleep and the energies are not needed during the day), autonomous or activateable. Autonomous programmes are effective where a crystal will be needed continuously for a particular task or purpose over a long period of time (such as to break a bad habit), whereas activateable programmes are more suited to crystals that will be worked with as and when needed.

If the crystal is to be programmed to emit positive energy vibrations over a long period of time, it is important to build into the programme an element of self-cleansing and clearing, stating that the crystal will not hold onto nor become filled with the negative energies, but that it will release them to the Universe to be transformed into positive energies, and will be able to recharge itself with positive energies.

After grounding and centering, hold the base of the crystal in your Receiving Hand with the point facing away from your body and place your Sending Hand over the point of the crystal. Allow the energies of the Earth to rise up into your body from your feet, and the energies of the Universe or of white sparkling light to enter your body via the Crown Chakra and move downwards through your body until both energies mix within your Heart Chakra. Connect to the Deva of the crystal and once more ascertain if it is willing to be programmed for the purpose you intend. Wait for an answer, if it is affirmative then you may proceed. If the answer is no, ask the crystal whether it is willing to work with you, how it is willing to work with you, and for what purpose.

Begin to visualise the programme or the crystal in terms of any colours, images, thoughts or feelings; and speak, sing or chant any words you have formulated for the programme, and begin to move the energy from your Heart Chakra, via your Sending Hand, into the crystal. Continue to maintain this focus for as long as it feels right to do so, and until the crystal is vibrant and pulsing with energy. When you sense that the crystal is fully programmed, state that the programme is now locked within the crystal, and is in accordance with the highest good for all. Release any excess energies back to the Earth or the Universe, thank the crystal, and ground your energies once more.

The crystal used to direct energy in Crystal Healing will need to be programmed to act as a conduit for healing energy from the Earth and the Universe using an activateable programme. To activate any crystal programmed in this way, hold it in your Sending Hand with the point away from you, and place your Receiving Hand over the point. Intend that the programme within the crystal be activated.

Crystal clusters are programmed in much the same way, either as a whole, or as individual points within the cluster, provided that the programmes work in harmony with each other. Tumbled stones and other polished stones are programmed in the same way as for crystal points, with one hand above and one below the stone.

Crystals may be programmed:

To hold a message or thought pattern
To work for a specific purpose
To broadcast affirmations, energies
To enhance protection
To emit energies of a particular colour
To act as a conduit for healing energies
To act as a template upon which other crystals may be
   programmed
To enhance positive attributes.

These are some of the limitless purposes crystals can be programmed for. Crystals may also be programmed for other people with the intended recipient's permission. During the programming process, visualise the intended recipient receiving the beneficial energies from the crystal.

Exercise: Programming a Crystal

You will need one cleansed and charged Quartz crystal that you have selected as your working partner in Crystal Healing. This crystal will be a conduit for healing energies, and will direct the flow of energy as required during the Crystal Healing session. An example of the words to use in programming this crystal is:

"Healing Energy Conduit, Direct the Flow of Energy As Needed."

The energy colour can be visualised as golden white, pure white, sparkling and bright, or as whatever colour you associate with the flow of pure, healing energy.

As detailed above, ascertain if the crystal is willing to accept this programme, and if so, proceed. Record your experiences.

Practice activating the crystal, and sending energy through it. Record your experiences.

De-Programming (also called Disenchanting) Crystals

Where a programme within a crystal has taken effect, such as in the breaking of a bad habit, the crystal will need to be de-programmed, before cleansing and charging in the normal way. To de-programme a crystal, firstly ground and centre yourself, then hold the base of the crystal in your Receiving Hand with the point facing away from your body and place your Sending Hand over the point of the crystal. Allow the energies of the Earth to rise up into your body from your feet, and the energies of the Universe or of white sparkling light to enter your body via the Crown Chakra and move downwards through your body until both energies mix within your Heart Chakra. Connect to the Deva of the crystal and begin to visualise the programme dissolving from within the crystal. Move the energy from your Heart Chakra, via your Sending Hand, into the crystal, continuing to dissolve the programme, until you feel it has disappeared entirely. Maintain this focus for as long as it feels right to do so, and until the crystal feels cleared. Inwardly or aloud, state that the crystal is now cleared, and release any excess energies back to the Earth or the Universe. Ground your energies once more.

18. Chakra Energy Assessment

Before any Crystal Healing work can commence, the energy status of each of the Chakras needs to be ascertained, either by dowsing with a pendulum or sensing with the hands.

Wide Circles

If the pendulum swings in wide circles, this indicates that the Chakra is too open, and therefore vulnerable to all kinds of energy passing into it, unable to protect itself against negative energy, and unable to retain energy.

A Chakra that is too open will need closing to an appropriate functional level, and protecting. Chakras should never be closed completely, as this will prevent any energy passing through them at all. If a Chakra is visualised as a flower, then its appropriate level of openness for everyday life would be as a bud with one petal open.

Little or No Movement

If the pendulum only swings in a small circle, or has no movement at all, this indicates that the Chakra is too closed, or that the energy level of that Chakra is depleted.

A Chakra that is too closed will need opening to an appropriate level, and the instilling of positive energy to build and strengthen it.

Where the energy of a Chakra is depleted or absent, positive energy will need to be instilled into it.

Negative Energy

The pendulum can then be asked to indicate whether there is negative energy accumulated within the Chakra, using the yes/no responses. Negative energy will also feel "wrong", sticky or tingly in an uncomfortable way when you run your sensing hand over it.

Energy Blockages

Energy blockages in the Chakras can be detected with the pendulum in the same way as for negative energy. Energy blockages can also be detected with your sensing hand, and will feel either hotter or colder than the surrounding areas of the body.

Negative energy accumulation and energy blockages in the Chakras will need clearing, to disperse the built up or blocked energies, and then will need instilling with positive energy, before being balanced.

The Chakra will then need to be closed to an appropriate functional level.

Once all the Chakras have been assessed for their energy status, the rest of the body can be scanned, either with a pendulum, or with your sensing hand, to detect any anomalies in the energy. Some people prefer to use only their hands to do this, it does become easier with practice.

When scanning the body with the pendulum to detect energy anomalies, allow the pendulum to hang as still as possible, and slowly move it up one side of the body and down the other side. Anomalies in the body's energy field will be apparent as movement of, or differences in the swing of the pendulum. The nature of each anomaly can then be determined using the yes/no swing of the pendulum. Make a note of the location and the nature of any energy anomalies found.

Scanning the body using the hands is done in much the same way, using the pendulum if necessary as a back up to confirm any sensations and determine their nature.

Once the assessment of the Chakras and the body's energy has been completed, make a note of what action to undertake for each Chakra and for each of the accumulations or blockages of energy found.

Dispersing Blocked Energy and Instilling Positive Energy

Where accumulations of negative energy or energy blockages have been detected, these need to be dispersed using a quartz crystal (as described in the section on Energy). Once the energy has been moved or removed in this way, positive energy needs to be instilled into the Chakra or location using the quartz crystal point as a conduit for energy.

Slowly work your way through any energy blockages and accumulations of negative energy, first drawing out or moving the energy, and then instilling positive energy. Then dowse the Chakras and scan the body to ascertain the energy status of each Chakra and any other areas that were previously drawn to your attention due to energy imbalances.

Balancing The Chakra Energies

Using your hands, or a smooth polished stone in each hand (such as a sphere) to amplify the energy, begin to balance the Chakra energies, working with two at a time. Hold your hands in the body's energy field, approximately 2 to 3 inches above the body, and focus on feeling the energies, and push them up or down as needed, to achieve a balanced level. Begin with the Crown Chakra and Throat Chakra, Then work down the body in the following pairs: Third Eye Chakra and Heart Chakra, Throat Chakra and Solar Plexus Chakra, Heart Chakra and Sacral Chakra, Solar Plexus and Base Chakra. If you are working on the Thymus Chakra, balance it with the Crown Chakra, after the Throat Chakra has been balanced, and with the Sacral Chakra before the Heart Chakra has been balanced.

Scan the whole of the body's energy field using your Sensing Hand held approximately 2 to 3 inches above the body, or by dowsing with a pendulum. If there are any areas that feel wrong or "sticky", accumulations of energy, energy depleted areas, or any areas of disharmonious energy; these can be dealt with by placing an appropriate stone on the area (either dowse for the correct one, choose intuitively, or use clear quartz), and using a quartz crystal to draw out or to instill energy.

Exercise: Chakra Assessment with the pendulum

NOTE: Chakra assessment may be done on oneself, or with the assistance of a friend.

Tools: Pendulum (preferably Quartz or Amethyst)

Hold the pendulum point approximately 2 to 3 inches above the body. Beginning at the Base (Root) Chakra, dowse for that Chakra's energy status. Make a note of whether each Chakra is too open, too closed, or balanced. Then dowse, using the yes or no swings of the pendulum, for whether there is an accumulation of negative energy, an energy blockage, energy depletion, or sufficient, positive energy. Make a note of this. Repeat for each of the Chakras, working up the body. Then, using either the pendulum or your sensing hand, scan the body for any energy anomalies. Make a note of the location and the nature of anything found, as before.

Exercise: Chakra Energy Assessment with the hands

Instead of using a pendulum, repeat the exercise above, using your sensing hand to determine the energy status of each Chakra in turn, and then scan the body. Make notes of your findings, and any impressions, images, feelings, words or thoughts you have that seem significant.

Which method you use to assess the energy status of the Chakras is very much a matter of personal choice and with practice will become second nature.

Exercise: Balancing Chakra Energy

Once any energy blockages, accumulations of negative energy or energy deficiencies have been located, use the appropriate method to rebalance and restore positive energy to these locations. Dowse the Chakras and any other previously unbalanced area after doing so, and scan the whole body before commencing Chakra Balancing.

Record your experiences of moving energy and restoring balance.

Expansion of Chakra Energies and Spiritual Growth

The energies of the Chakras can also be expanded and transformed to a higher level of vibration. This is a more advanced level of spiritual work, and should only be undertaken as part of a planned progression of spiritual growth, done carefully, thoughtfully, and gradually, to avoid causing any discomfort, harm or imbalance resulting from attempting to progress too far too fast.

Expansion and transformation of the Chakra energies will use highly evolved spiritual stones, which tend to have great clarity and powerful vibrational energies.

19. Meditation Layout for Energising the Chakras

This meditation and crystal layout opens the Chakras, draws in and retains positive energy, then closes the Chakras to an appropriate functional level. It is simple, yet powerful, and should have an energising and balancing effect on your whole being.

The meditation can be used separately from the crystal layout, but the addition of the vibrational energies of the crystals has a deepening effect and enlivens the experience.

Tools: Cleansed and charged tumbled stones of the appropriate colour (or type) for each Chakra – a possible selection is as follows:

Red Jasper (Base (Root) Chakra – one or two stones.

Carnelian (Sacral Chakra).

Citrine (Solar Plexus Chakra).

Green Aventurine (Heart Chakra).

(Optional – Amazonite (Thymus Chakra)).

Blue Lace Agate (Throat Chakra).

Sodalite (Third Eye (Brow) Chakra).

Amethyst (Crown Chakra).

Rose Quartz – two stones.

and

One Quartz crystal point and one Smokey Quartz point.

In a warm and safe place, where you have sufficient space to lie down comfortably (e.g. on your bed), and at a time when you will not be disturbed for at least an hour, carefully arrange the crystals in the following order:

Before you lie down, place the Quartz Point above where your head will be, with the point towards you, and place the Smokey Quartz below your feet with the point also towards you. Then lie down so that you are aligned with the two crystals. Ideally, you world be aligned North-South, with your head in the North (reverse this for the Southern Hemisphere) to line up with the magnetic polarity of the Earth.

Place one Red Jasper on your Base (Root) Chakra, or one stone at the top of each leg.

Place Carnelian on your Sacral Chakra.

Place Citrine on your Solar Plexus Chakra.

Place Green Aventurine on your Heart Chakra.

(Optional – Place Amazonite on your Thymus Chakra).

Place Blue Lace Agate on your Throat Chakra.

Place Sodalite on your Third Eye (Brow) Chakra.

Place Amethyst at your Crown Chakra.

Hold a Rose Quartz in each of your hands.

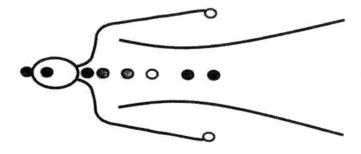

Allow yourself to relax, and take a few long, slow, deep
breaths.

Feel the gentle pink energies of the Rose Quartz stones in
your hands expand outwards, until your hands are filled with
a glowing pink light. As you breathe in, allow this light to flow
outwards and to fill your whole being. When you are filled
with the gentle pink light, take a few slow, deep breaths and
expand the pink light to surround you.

Visualise your Base Chakra as a bright red flower bud, at the
base of your spine. As the petals of the flower open, it becomes
a more vibrant red colour. Each time you breathe in, red light
flows outwards from your Base Chakra, expanding to fill your
whole being. When you are filled with this radiant red light,
take a few slow, deep breaths and expand the red light to
surround and protect you.

Move on to your Sacral Chakra, seeing a glowing orange
flower bud just below your navel, gently opening its petals
and beginning to spread a warm orange light through your
body. Each time you breathe in, the orange glow becomes
brighter, warmer and more comforting, and it expands to fill
your whole being. When you are completely filled with this

warm orange light, take a few slow, deep breaths and expand the orange light to surround and to nurture you.

Now move to your Solar Plexus Chakra, seeing a clear yellow flower bud at the base of your ribcage, in the centre of your body. As the flower opens its petals, it becomes brighter and brighter yellow. Each time you breathe in, the bright yellow light floods outwards, filling your whole being. When you are filled with bright yellow light, take a few slow, deep breaths and expand the yellow light to surround and energise you.

Move on to your Heart Chakra, visualising a natural green flower bud, in your heart, at the centre of your chest. As the petals of the flower open, it becomes a more vibrant green colour. Each time you breathe in, green light flows outwards from your Heart Chakra, expanding to fill your whole being. When you are filled with this vivid green light, take a few slow, deep breaths and expand the green light to surround and heal you.

(Optional - Now move to your Thymus Chakra, seeing a bright turquoise flower bud above your Thymus Gland, between your heart and throat. As the flower opens its petals, it becomes a more vibrant turquoise colour. Each time you breathe in, the bright turquoise light floods outwards, filling your whole being. When you are filled with bright turquoise light, take a few slow, deep breaths and expand the turquoise light to surround and energise you).

Now move on to your Throat Chakra, seeing a glowing sky blue flower bud at your throat, gently opening its petals and beginning to spread a clear blue light through your body. Each time you breathe in, the blue light becomes clearer and brighter, and it expands to fill your whole being. When you are completely filled with this clear blue light, take a few slow, deep breaths and expand the blue light to surround and to reassure you.

Move to your Third Eye Chakra, seeing a vibrant indigo flower bud at in the centre of your forehead, just above your eyes. As the flower opens its petals, it begins to spread an indigo glow through your body. Each time you breathe in, the indigo light floods outwards, filling your whole being. When you are filled with indigo light, take a few slow, deep breaths and expand the indigo light to surround and connect you.

Now move on to your Crown Chakra, visualising a deep violet flower bud, at your crown, at the top of your head. As the petals of the flower open, it becomes a richer violet colour. Each time you breathe in, violet light flows outwards from your Crown Chakra, expanding to fill your whole being. When you are filled with this deep violet light, take a few slow, deep breaths and expand the violet light to surround and enlighten you.

Now that all your Chakras are opened and energised, take a few long, slow, deep breaths. Begin to draw into yourself a brilliant sparkling white light, beginning from the centre of your being, and expanding outwards. Each time you breathe in, the sparkling white light fills and energises you until you are overflowing with light.

Focus on your Crown Chakra, and begin to close the petals of the violet flower, taking in enough sparkling white light to keep it energised, and leaving one petal open.

Move down to your Third Eye Chakra, drawing in enough light to keep it energised as the petals of the indigo flower close, leaving one petal open.

Focus on your Throat Chakra, and begin to close the petals of the sky blue flower, taking in enough sparkling white light to keep it energised, and leaving one petal open.

(Optional - Focus on your Thymus Chakra, drawing in enough turquoise light to keep it energised, as the petals of the turquoise flower close, leaving one petal open).

Move down to your Heart Chakra, drawing in enough light to keep it energised as the petals of the green flower close, leaving one petal open.

Focus on your Solar Plexus Chakra, and begin to close the petals of the yellow flower, taking in enough sparkling white light to keep it energised, and leaving one petal open.

Move down to your Sacral Chakra, drawing in enough light to keep it energised as the petals of the orange flower close, leaving one petal open.

Focus now on your Base Chakra, and begin to close the petals of the red flower, taking in enough sparkling white light to keep it energised, and leaving one petal open.

Take a few long, slow, deep breaths, and open your eyes. Give yourself time to become aware of your surroundings before sitting up. Hold the Smokey quartz point in your receiving hand for a few minutes, with the point towards you. This will help to ground your energies, and to return you to the waking world.

Cleanse and charge all the crystals used.

FuRtheR WoRk

1. Practice this meditation once a week, if possible. Record your experiences.

2. Using the sequence as a guide, write your own meditation for opening, energising and closing the Chakras. Record your experiences of using this meditation.

20. Meditation and Crystal Layout for Clearing Blocked and Negative Energy

This crystal layout and meditation is used to get your energies moving, and to clear blocked or negative energy. The placement of the crystals forms a six-pointed star, made from two interlocking triangles.

Tools: Six small cleansed and charged Quartz points.

In a warm and safe place, where you have sufficient space to lie down comfortably (e.g. on your bed), and at a time when you will not be disturbed for at least an hour, carefully arrange the crystals.

Before you lie down, place the small Quartz points in a circle that is large enough to surround your body in the following order:

One crystal above your head, point outwards.

One crystal point to the outside of your left knee, point towards your head.

One crystal point to the outside of your right knee, point towards your head. This completes the first triangle.

One crystal point below your feet, point towards your head.

One crystal point to the outside of your right elbow, point towards your head.

One crystal point to the outside of your left elbow, point towards your head. This completes the second, interlocking triangle.

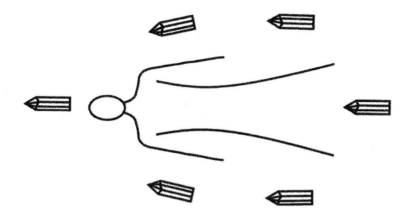

Lay down so that you are aligned with the head and feet crystals. Allow yourself to relax, and take a few long, slow, deep breaths.

Visualise a beam of sparkling white light slowly connecting the crystals in the following pattern:

Head to left knee.

Left knee to right knee.

Right knee to head.

Head to feet, connecting with the crystals at your left elbow and left knee along the way.

Feet to right elbow.

Right elbow to left elbow.

Left elbow to feet.

Feet to head, connecting with the crystals at your right knee and right elbow along the way.

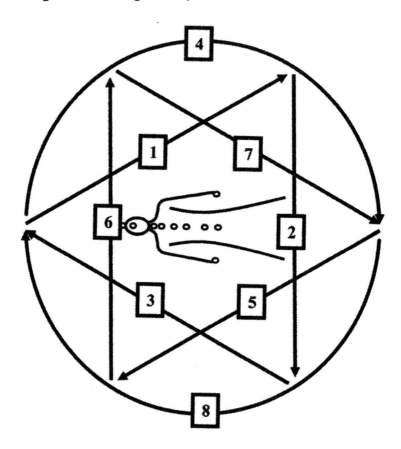

Slowly repeat the connection path of the crystals seven times. Feel the energies of the crystals and the sparkling white light all around you.

Relax and breathe slowly and deeply.

When you are ready to awaken, take a few long, slow, deep breaths, and open your eyes. Give yourself time to become aware of your surroundings before sitting up.

It is a good idea to hold a grounding stone, such as Haematite or Smokey Quartz in your receiving hand for a few minutes after this meditation, with the point towards you. This will help to ground your energies, and to return you to the waking world.

FuRtheR WoRk

1. Practice this meditation once a week, if possible. Record your experiences.

2. Follow this meditation with the Chakra stone meditation you have written. Record your experiences.

3. This meditation and crystal layout can be used for a more powerful energy clearing layout, by arranging all the Quartz points to face outwards and proceeding with the rest of the meditation. This MUST be followed immediately with an energising and balancing crystal layout or meditation, such as the Chakra stone meditation.

Likewise if the crystals are arranged with all the points facing inwards, it will have an energising effect, so it is preferable that an energy clearing meditation and crystal layout precedes it.

Record your experiences of these two variations of the crystal layout.

21. Crystal Energy Grids

Crystal energy grids are crystal layouts for a particular purpose such as distant healing, manifestation or protection. The crystals are laid out in the form of a six-pointed star, with a stone or crystal in the centre as the focus of the grid. The outer crystals are then connected using the Generator crystal, both in the pattern previously described in the clearing layout, and then each of the outer crystals in turn, moving clockwise round from the first crystal, is connected via the central crystal or stone while the intention of the grid is visualised.

The pattern for connecting the crystals and the centre is as follows: From one outer crystal to the centre and back again. Move across clockwise to the next outer crystal and repeat. Continue until the connection is complete, and repeat the whole circle seven times, or as many as feels intuitively right.

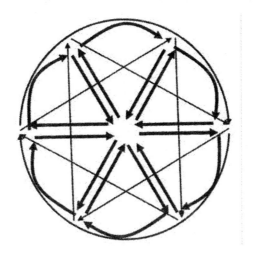

The stone in the centre of the grid can represent a person to whom healing energies are being directed. If this is the case, the flow of healing energy should be focussed onto the central stone, while the intended recipient is strongly visualised as being healed and whole.

If the intention of the grid is to assist in manifesting or achieving something, a piece of paper with the desired result written on it can be placed beneath the central stone. The outer crystals are connected and the desired outcome is strongly visualised whilst energy is being directed towards it. State inwardly or aloud that the desired result will be for the highest good of all.

22. Gem Waters and Gem Essences

WARNING: Some crystals, rocks, minerals and gemstones are poisonous if ingested! Stones containing copper, mercury, arsenic, iron, cobalt, lead, asbestos or are radioactive are DEFINITELY NOT recommended for use in preparation of Gem Waters and Gem Essences in the direct way. For stones containing the above metals, or for any where the chemical composition is not known, use the Indirect Preparation Method detailed below. Use of radioactive minerals in Crystal Healing is NOT RECOMMENDED in any way.

Gem Waters

Direct Preparation Method:
To prepare a Gem Water, place a clean, cleansed and charged crystal in a clean glass or non-metallic container, add enough pure spring water to cover the crystal, and leave it in sunlight or moonlight (or neither) for up to twelve hours. The water should then be strained (for example through a coffee filter paper). Gem Waters can be kept in the refrigerator for up to three days before being discarded.

Gem Waters can be used to water plants, added to the bath, consumed on their own or in combination with other healing substances, added to food, etc. They should be looked upon as a tonic, to increase health and well-being.

Gem Elixírs or Essences

Direct Preparation Method:
Gem Essences (also called Gem Elixirs) are prepared in much the same way as Gem Waters. They can be thought of as an energy medicine, and should not be used frivolously.

A few small dark-coloured glass bottles with dropper caps are sterilised by heating in water until boiling for a few minutes. The bottles are drained and allowed to cool with the caps loosely fitted.

A clean, cleansed and charged, programmed crystal is placed in a glass or non-metallic container and covered with pure spring water. The crystal Deva is asked to charge the water and imbue it with healing energies for a particular purpose (whatever the Essence is being created for). The water is then left in sunlight or moonlight (or both, or neither) for up to 24 hours. The water should then be strained (for example through a clean coffee filter paper) and used to half-fill the prepared bottles. Each bottle is then topped up with an alcohol such as brandy, to act as a preservative. The bottles should then be tightly capped and shaken well before use. Gem Essences will keep for up to six months, if stored in a dark place. Any Gem Essence which is surplus to requirements (before the addition of the alcohol) should be returned to the Earth, with thanks.

Gem Essences can also be preserved with honey, if alcohol is inappropriate, by adding a teaspoonful to each bottle and shaking well to mix. They will only keep for about one month, and should be stored in the refrigerator.

Indirect Preparation Method for Gem Waters and Gem Essences:
Place a small glass or non-metallic container inside a larger glass or non-metallic container. Add pure spring water to the

larger container, to about halfway up the sides of the smaller container. Add the crystal to the smaller container, and ask the crystal Deva to charge the water and imbue it with healing energies.

Taking Gem Essences

To take a Gem Essence, add a few drops to a glass of spring water, or take a number of drops under the tongue. The appropriate amount of drops, and the frequency and duration of use can be determined by dowsing for the answers with a pendulum.

Combination Stone Essences

Gem Essences can be made using a combination of crystals, for example a Chakra Balancing Essence could comprise the energies of Red Jasper, Carnelian, Citrine, Aventurine, Blue Lace Agate, Lapis Lazuli and Amethyst. Each crystal would need cleansing, charging and programming for the purpose intended, and their energies combined in the water.

Exercise 1: Using the direct preparation methods detailed above, and a clean, cleansed and charged Quartz crystal, make some Gem Water to drink over the next three days. Record your experiences. Make Gem Water using Amethyst, to drink on the following three days. Again, record your experiences. Do you notice any differences in the effects of the Gem waters?

Exercise 2: Using the direct preparation method detailed above, and a clean, cleansed and charged Rose Quartz tumbled stone, make a Gem Essence. Decide on an appropriate purpose for the Essence, programme the crystal and work with its Deva accordingly. Record your experiences.

Using a pendulum, dowse the correct dosage, frequency and duration for you to take this Gem Essence. Record any experiences you have whilst taking the Essence.

Exercise 3: Using the indirect preparation method detailed above, and a clean, cleansed and charged Haematite tumbled stone, prepare a Gem Essence (be careful to keep the stone separate from the water!). Decide on an appropriate purpose for the Essence, programme the crystal and work with its Deva accordingly. Record your experiences. Using a pendulum, dowse the correct dosage, frequency and duration for you to take this Gem Essence. Record any experiences you have whilst taking the Essence.

Exercise 4: Using the appropriate method(s) as detailed above, create a Gem Essence using a combination of stones appropriate to a particular purpose. Record the stones used, the method(s) used, and your experiences. Using a pendulum, dowse the correct dosage, frequency and duration for you to take this Gem Essence. Record any experiences you have whilst taking the Essence.

Part 3

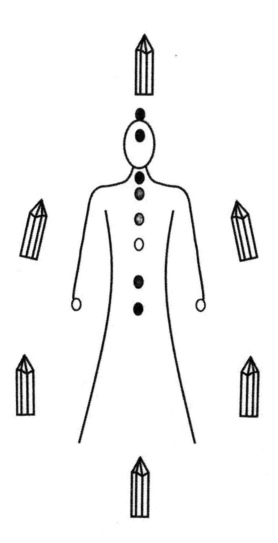

Dírectory of Crystal Properties

Stone: Agate – Blue Lace Agate
Usual Colour: Pale blue, striped or banded with a lace pattern
Physical: Soothing and beneficial
Emotional: Peace and gentleness
Mental: Calmness; clear mind; awareness
Spiritual: Inspiration and attunement; higher state of awareness
Magical: Peace; happiness

Stone: Agate – Botswana Agate
Usual Colour: Banded grey to greyish brown, black and white
Physical: Removal of toxins; improves health and strength; pain relief; healing
Emotional: Eternal love and fidelity; confidence and self-confidence; removes stress
Mental: Attention to detail; vigilance; conscientiousness; alleviates depression
Spiritual: Energises the auric field; cleanses, balances and regenerates; removes energy blockages; grounding
Magical: Energy; protection; stability; to attract love; to stop smoking

Stone: Agate – Green Moss Agate
Usual Colour: Translucent white to clear, with green moss-like veins
Physical: Alleviates colds, flu and fungal infections; relieves dehydration; improves speed
Emotional: Agreeability; emotional balancing
Mental: Positivity and persuasiveness; agreeability; self esteem
Spiritual: Use to attune with Nature spirits, faeries, devas

Magical: Abundance; gardening; wealth

Stone: Amazonite
Usual Colour: Green to greenish blue, usually with white striations
Physical: Eases problems with the nervous system
Emotional: Balances and calms the emotions
Mental: Clarity; tranquillity; harmony
Spiritual: Balance; accessing distant memories and ancestral knowledge
Magical: Tranquillity; harmony

Stone: Amber
Usual Colour: Translucent honey colours, from cream to golden brown
Physical: Enhances beauty; eases headache; brings warmth
Emotional: Calming and comforting
Mental: Restores memory loss
Spiritual: Protection; energising
Magical: Good luck; life energy; connection with solar energies

Stone: Amethyst
Usual Colour: Purple, all shades from darkest violet to pale lavender
Physical: Can relieve headaches and insomnia; promotes invigoration and restful sleep; to get rid of addictions
Emotional: Defuses anger; brings calm and balance; for love, peace and friendship; releases jealousy
Mental: Helps sharpen the mind; improves memory and brings new ideas; for interviews; relieves stress
Spiritual: For energy balancing and tranquillity; enhances psychic awareness
Magical: Protects against psychic attack and danger; drives off nightmares; to remember dreams; for healing; calm; love; peace

Stone: Ametrine
Usual Colour: Purple and golden yellow-orange, sometimes with clear in between
Physical: Helps with the immune system; energises
Emotional: Clears emotional blockages and stress; has a stabilising effect
Mental: Stimulates creativity; assists in overcoming prejudices; development of consciousness
Spiritual: Enhances higher states of awareness; raises levels of consciousness; dispels negativity
Magical: For peace, tranquillity, balance and universal equilibrium

Stone: Angelite
Usual Colour: Semi-translucent pale greyish to sky blue
Physical: Eases throat complaints
Emotional: Soothes the emotions; alleviates confusion
Mental: Calms the thoughts; improves attention span; improves communication
Spiritual: Connection with angelic and other benevolent energies; peace
Magical: peace; calm; connection to benevolent energies
Note: Do not leave in water for long periods of time as this can damage the stone

Stone: Apatite
Usual Colour: Translucent green, yellow or blue
Physical: Can suppress hunger
Emotional: Dissolves aloofness
Mental: Clears mental confusion
Spiritual: For deep meditation; to promote feelings of oneness
Magical: For past life recall; healing
Note: fragile, may be damaged by harder stones

Stone: Apophyllite
Usual Colour: Brilliantly clear or pale translucent green
Physical: Maintains energy levels for preservation and rejuvenation
Emotional: Brings the energies of light and love
Mental: For clarity and focus
Spiritual: Facilitates astral travel; intuitive vision; connects to Universal love
Magical: For use in energy charging; scrying
Note: fragile, may be damaged by harder stones

Stone: Aquamarine
Usual Colour: Translucent blue-green
Physical: Eases swollen glands; enhances peaceful sleep and relaxation
Emotional: For courage; to release guilt; for peace
Mental: Enhances intellectual awareness
Spiritual: Shields the aura; for attunement and psychic awareness; purification and protection from negativity
Magical: Karma; healing humanity; peace; courage; purification; protection

Stone: Aventurine – Green Aventurine
Usual Colour: Green with random sparkly flakes
Physical: Speeds healing and can help strengthen muscles, eyes, lungs and heart; Eases migraine, neuralgia and flu
Emotional: Calms and clears, allowing empathy
Mental: Amplifies leadership qualities and decisiveness; for independence, focus, study and creativity; to remember dreams
Spiritual: Provides an energy shield; nurtures instinct
Magical: For abundance, creativity and luck in games of chance; for increased focus; success; prosperity; independence; travel; money and wealth; to stop smoking or overeating

Stone: Bloodstone
Usual Colour: Solid green with flecks of red
Physical: Can help stop the flow of blood from wounds; helps
alleviate fever
Emotional: Assists with unselfishness; friendship and
relationships; courage and bravery
Mental: For courage; gives practical wisdom and sensitivity
Spiritual: To renew, ground and balance energy; to be fully
present in the here and now; for protection
Magical: For health, vitality, courage, wisdom, harmony;
business success; interviews and employment; grounding;
protection

Stone: Calcite – Iceland Spar
Usual Colour: Clear, with double-refraction
Physical: For energy; can relieve pain
Emotional: Releases guilt; alleviates stress
Mental: Assists with study; focuses direction in life; helps
with communication
Spiritual: Purification, healing and energy; Cleansing and
clearing
Magical: Energy; purification; healing; direction
Note: fragile, may be damaged by harder stones

Stone: Carnelian
Usual Colour: Orange-red, semi-translucent
Physical: Can stimulate sexual impulses; increases energy
Emotional: Protects against envy, sorrow, fear and rage;
brings courage and a love of life; strengthens family love and
unity; sex and passion
Mental: Stops nightmares; sharpens concentration and
analytical precision; increases inquisitiveness
Spiritual: Strengthens astral vision; for inspiration and
connectedness
Magical: For protection, confidence, sexual energy and
courage; abundance; protection during travel; performance
in interviews

Stone: Celestite
Usual Colour: Translucent to clear pale blue
Physical: Assists with calm relaxation
Emotional: Brings hope; calmness; pleasantness
Mental: Dismisses worries; creativity and the arts
Spiritual: Healing and balance; assists with astral travel
Magical: Hope; healing; balance; calm
Note: fragile, may be damaged by harder stones

Stone: Chalcedony – Blue Chalcedony
Usual Colour: Translucent grey-blue
Physical: Helps the body with mineral assimilation
Emotional: Benevolence
Mental: Can increase mental stability
Spiritual: Encourages brotherhood among all
Magical: For protection during travel

Stone: Charoite
Usual Colour: Purple with inclusions of white and black
Physical: Can help transmute illness to wellness
Emotional: Enhances unconditional love; reduces worry
Mental: Improves observation, scrutiny, analysis and
  investigation
Spiritual: Gives spiritual insight; synthesis between heart
  and crown Chakras
Magical: For transformation; visions; second sight

Stone: Chrysocolla
Usual Colour: Blue-green in varied patterns and swirls
Physical: Regenerative and strengthening
Emotional: Increases the capacity to love; for inner strength;
  releases jealousy; reduces insecurity; friendship
Mental: For the intellect and communication
Spiritual: For attunement to the Earth; psychic development;
  enhances meditation; harmony
Magical: Attracts love; psychic development; home
  purification; friendship; harmony; healing

Note: Do not use in direct-method gem elixirs as this stone contains copper

Stone: Chrysoprase
Usual Colour: Apple green
Physical: To increase dexterity; for peaceful sleep
Emotional: Fidelity and compassion; friendship
Mental: For presence of mind; for acceptance of self, others and life
Spiritual: Aligns the Chakras with the ethereal plane
Magical: Attracts success; luck; protection; fidelity in love and in business; friendship

Stone: Citrine
Usual Colour: Clear golden yellow
Physical: For improving circulation and increasing energy; helps the digestive system; can ease diabetes
Emotional: Enhances comfort; cheerfulness, optimism and confidence
Mental: Enhances creativity and concentration; allows for a studious and focused mind; for problem-solving; clarity and clear-thinking
Spiritual: Balancing; allows one to be generous and sharing; for psychic dreams
Magical: For abundance; transactions involving money; removes fear; to acquire and maintain wealth; clarity; protection

Stone: Chiastolite
Usual Colour: Brownish pink with a distinctive cross configuration
Physical: Can lessen fear
Emotional: Assists during change
Mental: Creativity and practicality; for a balanced perspective; to gain insight
Spiritual: Death and rebirth; protection against curses and negativity

125

Magical: Protection against curses and negativity; death and rebirth

Stone: Danburite
Usual Colour: Clear and sparkling, sometimes tinges with pink or lilac
Physical: Has a detoxifying action
Emotional: Nurtures the heart energy; supports strength through troubled times
Mental: Improves mental powers and releases mental imperatives
Spiritual: Brings serenity; enhances spiritual growth
Magical: For strength; access to eternal wisdom; a karmic cleanser

Stone: Dumortierite
Usual Colour: Grey blue, with darker flecks
Physical: For stamina in harsh environments; to understand the underlying cause of a disease or condition
Emotional: Helps one stand up for oneself; assists with relationships
Mental: Patience; reduces stubbornness; reduces excitability
Spiritual: Helps maintain equilibrium
Magical: To resolve opposites into unity; equilibrium; balance

Stone: Emerald
Usual Colour: Deep bright green
Physical: Can help improve eyesight; relieves headaches; enhances beauty
Emotional: Successful love;
Mental: For intelligence and improved memory; relieves depression
Spiritual: For psychic awareness
Magical: Psychic awareness; study; successful love

Stone: Fluorite

Usual Colour: Banded translucent purple, blue, green, yellow and clear

Physical: Speeds healing of colds and flu; can benefit teeth and bones; protection from illness

Emotional: Soothes depression, anger and desperation

Mental: Strengthens thoughts and reveals truth; enhances study and concentration

Spiritual: Grounds and integrates spiritual energies; for balance and equilibrium

Magical: Heightens intuitive mental powers; reveals the truth; to dissipate illness

Note: fragile, may be damaged by harder stones

Stone: Garnet

Usual Colour: Deep semi-translucent red

Physical: For strength and vigour, especially when exerting oneself; reduces laziness; stops overeating; improves health

Emotional: Enhances commitment and devotion to loved ones; for courage and self confidence

Mental: Allows self-discovery and rightness of will; reduces depression

Spiritual: Provides a shield to protect and strengthen the aura; Enhances clairvoyance

Magical: For strength, protection, courage, action, health and wellbeing

Stone: Haematite

Usual Colour: Dark metallic grey

Physical: Can draw out illness; supports the blood and kidneys; eases back pain; can strengthen the heart

Emotional: Allows acceptance; dissolves stress; brings happiness; kindness in love; courage

Mental: Enhances the willpower; gives patience

Spiritual: Provides grounding of energies

Magical: For protection; happiness; grounding; courage; for the home

Note: Do not use in direct-method gem elixirs

Stone: Iolite
Usual Colour: Translucent indigo, turns yellow on opposite axis
Physical: Promotes a strong constitution and respiratory system
Emotional: Enhances harmony and releases discord
Mental: Sharpens the intuitive mind
Spiritual: Assists shamanic experiences; expression of one's true self; enhances spiritual vision
Magical: For vision quests and out of body journeys; to restore harmony within the self

Stone: Jade
Usual Colour: Green to greyish green
Physical: Can ease kidney problems
Emotional: Brings love
Mental: For tact and diplomacy
Spiritual: Enhances connection to the ancestors and the spirits of the dead; respect and reverence for the ancestors
Magical: For money; to pay bills; brings luck; safe journeys and travel; respect for the ancestors; connection to the ancestors and the spirits of the dead

Stone: Jasper – Picture Jasper
Usual Colour: Buff, with veins and patterns of ochre, yellow and grey
Physical: Enhances the immune system
Emotional: To bring harmony; to allow for facing one's fears; brings suppressed emotions to the surface
Mental: Brings hidden thoughts to the surface; for creative visualisation
Spiritual: Enhances global awareness and Earth healing
Magical: For business; Nature; harmony

128

Stone: Jasper – Red Jasper
Usual Colour: Brick red
Physical: Can help alleviate fever and the effects of poison; increases beauty and grace; brings energy; increases appetite
Emotional: Nurtures; helps to rectify and resolve injustice
Mental: Helps one remember dreams that have real life connections
Spiritual: Helps one learn and progress in a focused and direct way; eliminates negativity; for grounding
Magical: Rain-making; defence; protection; strength; grounding; an amulet against evil; rescue from danger; justice; to prevent setbacks

Stone: Jet
Usual Colour: Black
Physical: Alleviates headaches, migraines and colds; protection from illness
Emotional: Calming
Mental: Dispels fearful thoughts; can lessen depression
Spiritual: Raises spiritual energy
Magical: For scrying, energy raising, ritual; business; finances; protection, especially from illness or violence; financial stability
Note: Jet will bond with its owner so will need careful cleansing

Stone: Kunzite
Usual Colour: Translucent pink to lilac
Physical: Assists in soothing joint pain
Emotional: Allows introspection; lifting mood
Mental: Enhances creativity; promotes tolerance
Spiritual: Activates the heart Chakra and balances all the energy centres
Magical: For peace, relaxation, calm; grounding

Stone: Kyanite
Usual Colour: Blue to grey-blue
Physical: Improves endurance; can help muscular disorders
Emotional: Allows one to speak the truth and to express love
Mental: Facilitates dream recall and intuition
Spiritual: Grounds and balances all the Chakras; for
meditation
Magical: Stimulates psychic abilities; for deep peace

Stone: Labradorite
Usual Colour: Grey-greenish with patches of brightly coloured
iridescence
Physical: Can help with eye and brain disorders
Emotional: Strengthens faith in the self
Mental: Banishes fears and insecurities from previous
disappointments; helps with shyness; for strength and
perseverance
Spiritual: Stimulates intuition and psychic gifts; for mystical,
psychic and intuitive wisdom
Magical: Facilitates initiation into the mysteries; for
beneficial transformation; destiny

Stone: Lapis Lazuli
Usual Colour: Royal blue with golden pyrite and white calcite
inclusions
Physical: Benefits the respiratory system; can improve health
Emotional: Releases one from negative emotional bondage;
brings hope
Mental: Amplifies thoughts; brings clarity and objectivity; can
ease depression; improves self confidence
Spiritual: Facilitates spiritual journeying; stimulates
personal spiritual power; for psychic dreams
Magical: For increased psychic awareness; courage; protection

Stone: Larimar
Usual Colour: Mottled sea-blue and white
Physical: Can draw out pain
Emotional: Facilitates the healing of trauma; creates equilibrium
Mental: Stimulates creativity and clarity of thought
Spiritual: Stimulates all the upper body Chakras
Magical: To dissolve energy blockages; to rebalance Earth energies

Stone: Leopardskin Rhyolite
Usual Colour: Mottled and spotted buff, brown earth colours
Physical: Helps dissipate skin disorders and rashes; raises energy and stamina
Emotional: Enhances self esteem and self worth; brings creativity and self realisation
Mental: Gives one strength to deal with everything calmly
Spiritual: Ignites the creativity of the soul
Magical: For past life healing; change and progress

Stone: Lepidolite
Usual Colour: Greyish purple with metallic flecks
Physical: Eases wrinkles; relieves tension; enhances self-preservation; can help during birth; enhances wellbeing
Emotional: For self-love and trust; alleviates despondency; allows acceptance of self and others; reduces stress
Mental: Enhances diplomacy; is calming and refreshing; improves business communication; releases sentimentality
Spiritual: Brings universal light and hope; smoothes during change, transition, birth and rebirth; releases energy blockages; assists astral travel
Magical: Rebirth; change; transformation; gardening abundance; transitions

Stone: Lodestone and Magnetite
Usual Colour: Dark metallic grey-black
Physical: For pain relief
Emotional: Releases stress
Mental: Improves motivation
Spiritual: Removes energy blockages
Magical: Draws or attracts, as directed
Note: Do not use in direct-method gem elixirs

Stone: Malachite
Usual Colour: Banded in different shades of green
Physical: Can enhance the immune system; relieves pain;
  eases vertigo
Emotional: Clarifying; alleviates shyness; allows the
  emotional healing of illness; relieves stress
Mental: Allows one to take responsibility; brings the qualities
  of fidelity and loyalty
Spiritual: Is transformative, clearing the Chakras; enhances
  psychic abilities
Magical: Protection during travel; business success; love;
  calm; wise use of money, resources and abundance
*Note: Do not use in direct-method gem elixirs as this stone
contains copper*

Stone: Moldavite
Usual Colour: Translucent greyish green
Physical: Supports the healing process; increases the flow of
  energy
Emotional: Helps with the expression and experience of love
Mental: Allows one to be unconventional, inspiring and
  inspired
Spiritual: Leads towards ascension and illumination;
  connection with higher beings, powers and entities; inter-
  connectedness
Magical: Travel to past and future lives; messages; clear
  visions; interconnection; other dimensions

Stone: Moonstone
Usual Colour: White, grey, pink or cream with an iridescent sheen
Physical: Sustains growth; can help with water balance; attunement to the body's cycles; fertility
Emotional: Alleviates tension; enhances creativity and self-expression; soothes the emotions; success and inspiration to lovers
Mental: For insight, perception, discernment and diplomacy
Spiritual: Allows for understanding of one's destiny; clears negativity
Magical: For love; wishing; fertility; divination; protection; Moon magic; attracts good things; success

Stone: Morganite
Usual Colour: Translucent pinkish
Physical: Helps alleviate breathing disorders
Emotional: Helps love to grow
Mental: Brings wisdom; calm mind
Spiritual: Brings emphasis of the equality between all things
Magical: for Earth healing; reverence

Stone: Nuumite
Usual Colour: Dark blackish blue, iridescent scales
Physical: Deepens relaxation; regenerative
Emotional: Reduces anxiety and stress
Mental: Can enhance memory
Spiritual: Aligns the Chakras; removes energy blockages; protects against negative energy; for intuition and insight; grounding and protective
Magical: connection with the ancient Earth; protection from negativity

Stone: Obsidian – Apache Tear
Usual Colour: Black, translucent grey-brown
Physical: Helps eliminate toxins from the body
Emotional: Eases grief; allows forgiveness

Mental: Stimulates precision and analytical abilities
Spiritual: Absorbs negative energy; protects the aura
Magical: For protection; comfort; gentle grounding; luck

Stone: Obsidian – Black Obsidian
Usual Colour: Black
Physical: Enhances healing
Emotional: Disperses unloving energies
Mental: Disperses negative thoughts
Spiritual: Allows connection to Earth energy; a shield against negativity; for inner and outer vision
Magical: for grounding; divination and scrying; visions; protection; to obtain a home

Stone: Obsidian – Snowflake Obsidian
Usual Colour: Black with white snowflake shapes at random
Physical: Enhances healing
Emotional: Gently soothing
Mental: Brings serenity in isolation
Spiritual: Protective and balancing; brings purity
Magical: Protection

Stone: Obsidian – Rainbow Obsidian
Usual Colour: Black, with bands of coloured iridescence
Physical: Can enhance healing
Emotional: Enhances enjoyment; brings the energies of light and love
Mental: Disperses negative thoughts
Spiritual: Allows for recognition of one's spiritual side
Magical: For pleasure, joy; protection

Stone: Onyx
Usual Colour: Black, or banded black and white
Physical: Can reduce sexual urges; for fidelity
Emotional: Banishes grief; can boost the ego and enhance self esteem; overcomes loneliness

Mental: Facilitates wise decision-making; for clear thinking; imagination; improves willpower; brings courage
Spiritual: Helps in following one's spiritual path
Magical: Use in defensive magic; to obtain a home; to attract good things; fidelity; willpower

Stone: Opal
Usual Colour: White with a play of colour
Physical: Can ease lung problems; enhances beauty; helps ease childbirth
Emotional: Calms nerves and temper; relieves anger
Mental: Calming
Spiritual: Allows one to fade into the background; facilitates psychic development
Magical: For beauty; happiness

Stone: Pearl
Usual Colour: White, peach, pink or cream with a pearlescent iridescence
Physical: Can increase fertility; for ease of childbirth
Emotional: Facilitates love
Mental: Enhances loyalty to a cause
Spiritual: For innocence, purity and faith
Magical: Love; loyalty; fertility; childbirth; connection to the Sea

Stone: Peridot
Usual Colour: Translucent pale to olive green
Physical: Can ease birth
Emotional: Heals a bruised ego; empowers love
Mental: Wards off delusions
Spiritual: Allows development of second sight
Magical: For power; witchcraft; employment; healing; protection

Stone: Pyrite
Usual Colour: Metallic gold
Physical: Can reduce fever and inflammation
Emotional: Personal power; expansive energy; empowerment
  to take action
Mental: Enhances intellect and improves memory
Spiritual: A shield from negativity
Magical: For money; prosperity; wealth; success; protection;
empowerment
Note: Do not use in direct-method gem elixirs

Stone: Quartz – Clear Quartz or Rock Crystal
Usual Colour: Clear to white, transparent or translucent
Physical: Energises; relieves pain; helps ease fever; for restful
  sleep; can reduce glandular swelling; for good health
Emotional: For self-acceptance and self-love; enhances
  intuition; brings courage
Mental: Brings clear focus; allows clarity of thought; conscious
  direction of energy; enhances awareness; concentration;
  assists with patience
Spiritual: For purification; harmony; alters consciousness;
  enhances psychic awareness; helps with astral projection
Magical: To bring rain; for healing; protection; power; energy;
  health; purification; to purify the home; for perseverance

Stone: Quartz – Herkimer Diamond Quartz
Usual Colour: Clear and sparkling
Physical: For relaxation; alleviates tension
Emotional: Removes fear
Mental: Clarity; helps with remembering and understanding
dreams
Spiritual: Attunement; clearing of energetic blockages
Magical: Clearing of negativity; conscious attunement and
connection

Stone: Quartz – Rose Quartz
Usual Colour: Pink, may be translucent
Physical: Nurtures the heart
Emotional: Enhances love, empathy and sensitivity; releases
guilt and jealousy
Mental: Promotes trust and harmony; inspires creativity
Spiritual: For attunement to loving energies; opens aware-
ness to the beauty of Nature; absorbs harmful vibrational
energies
Magical: To attract love, peace, happiness, friendship; to
strengthen marriage; for healing

Stone: Quartz – Rutilated Quartz
Usual Colour: Clear or cloudy with golden, brown or reddish
strands
Physical: Combats exhaustion and energy depletion;
alleviates bronchitis, asthma and chest complaints
Emotional: Helps one let go of the past
Mental: Can help ease depression; brings calmness, order and
stability
Spiritual: Draws off negative energy; facilitates astral travel
Magical: For use in scrying and divination; healing and
stability

Stone: Quartz – Smokey Quartz
Usual Colour: Brownish smoky to almost black, translucent or
opaque
Physical: Brings equilibrium to the body; brings pain relief
Emotional: Transforms negative emotions; elevates mood;
eases anger and resentment; improves self esteem
Mental: Can ease depression and worries; allows clarity of
thoughts
Spiritual: Activates survival instincts; balances energies;
grounding, stabilising and generally beneficial; protection
Magical: For grounding; protection; rebalancing; relieving
anger; helps frugality

Stone: Quartz – Tourmalinated Quartz
Usual Colour: Clear to cloudy with black strands and crystals
Physical: Enhances innate strength
Emotional: Facilitates smooth relationships
Mental: Helps with problem solving
Spiritual: Balances energies
Magical: A shield against negativity; for protection

Stone: Rhodochrosite
Usual Colour: Pink and rose-pink bands
Physical: Can assist in purifying the circulatory system
Emotional: Creates selfless love and compassion
Mental: For a dynamic and positive attitude
Spiritual: Expands consciousness
Magical: For energy; peace; love

Stone: Rhodonite
Usual Colour: Rose-pink with black inclusions and veins
Physical: Can enhance wound healing; can ease and assist
    with the elimination of skin disorders; helps with anaemia
Emotional: For emotional balance and clearing emotional
    wounds; for romance and love
Mental: Gives patience; dispels anxiety; eases worry; allows
    for an open mind; dispels confusion
Spiritual: Enhances meditation
Magical: For peace, calm; to cast off confusion or doubt

Stone: Ruby
Usual Colour: Bright to blood red
Physical: Improves strength; awakens sexual energy; reduces
    overeating
Emotional: Protects from unhappiness; brings a state of bliss;
    opens and energises the heart
Mental: For creativity
Spiritual: Brings protection from psychic attack
Magical: For the stability of wealth or abundance; protection;
    strength

Stone: Sapphire
Usual Colour: Blue to grey blue
Physical: Releases tension
Emotional: For intuition
Mental: Opens the mind to beauty, joy and peace; for discernment
Spiritual: For joy and the fulfilment of dreams
Magical: Prosperity; peace; intuition

Stone: Selenite
Usual Colour: White translucent with a sheen
Physical: Helps in alignment of the spinal column; assists with regeneration of cellular structure; can extend the lifespan; flexibility
Emotional: For peacefulness and calmness
Mental: Assists in telepathy; clarity of thought; improves good judgement; decreases reticence; improves flexibility of thought
Spiritual: Used in mysticism; for receiving higher guidance; can remove energy blockages; for clarity, insight and understanding
Magical: For reconciliation between lovers; awareness
Note: Selenite is water-soluble and fragile

Stone: Seraphinite
Usual Colour: Green, swirled with darker green and white
Physical: Helps release tension
Emotional: Opens the heart to love
Mental: Brings peace and fulfilment
Spiritual: For enlightenment
Magical: For out of body journeys; angelic connection

Stone: Sodalite
Usual Colour: Dark blue with greyer areas and white veining
Physical: Helps the immune system
Emotional: Improves self esteem; dispels guilt; brings peace

Mental: Enhances logical and rational mental processes; truthfulness; stimulates the intellect; promotes trust
Spiritual: For fellowship; living one's truth; brings a state of knowing
Magical: To dispel fear; for wisdom; healing; to still the mind

Stone: Sugilite
Usual Colour: Dark purple to black
Physical: Can ease headaches
Emotional: Allows forgiveness of self and others; eliminates hostility; improves self belief
Mental: For inspiration; confidence
Spiritual: Enhances spiritual love
Magical: Freedom; love

Stone: Tigereye – Gold Tigereye
Usual Colour: Banded shades of gold to brown with a play of light
Physical: Speeds healing, especially of broken bones; helps against hypochondria
Emotional: For calmness, confidence, optimism and courage
Mental: Enhances clear thinking; practicality; improves alertness
Spiritual: Heightens intuition and balances energies; protection
Magical: For grounding; abundance; protection; courage; luck; confidence; money; to pay bills; magical energy; enhancing psychic abilities; for interviews and employment; drives away evil

Stone: Tiger Iron
Usual Colour: Banded brick red, metallic grey and banded gold with a play of light
Physical: Improves vitality
Emotional: For courage and fortitude
Mental: Assists with creative endeavours or artistic ability
Spiritual: Protects from danger

140

Magical: A haven or refuge from danger
Note: Do not use in direct-method gem elixirs

Stone: Topaz
Usual Colour: Clear, greyish to blue, translucent
Physical: Assists in the healing of wounds; helps stop smoking
Emotional: For attraction and true love
Mental: Enables trusting in one's decisions; improves intellect
and reasoning ability; eases insomnia
Spiritual: Allows visualisation and manifestation
Magical: For abundance; safety of the home; for success in all
endeavours; assists in employment

Stone: Tourmaline – Black Tourmaline or Schorl
Usual Colour: Black
Physical: Increases healing and vitality; realigns the physical
body
Emotional: Helps diminish fear; promotes self confidence;
improves cheerfulness
Mental: To gain understanding; for practicality and creativity;
relieves anxiety and depression; brings inspiration
Spiritual: An energy shield to enhance wellbeing and block
negativity; immensely grounding
Magical: To cleanse; for grounding; psychic protection;
connection to the Earth; power; empowerment

Stone: Tourmaline – Watermelon Tourmaline
Usual Colour: Green to blue-green outside, pink core
Physical: Can alleviate heart and lung problems; stimulates
and energises
Emotional: Helps with sense of humour
Mental: Facilitates cooperation and tact; decreases
nervousness
Spiritual: Activate the heart Chakra; opens the spirit to the
beauty of Nature
Magical: For Nature; love; energy

Stone: Turquoise
Usual Colour: Blue-green
Physical: Can relieve headaches; helps release fevers
Emotional: Enhances love
Mental: Relieves insomnia
Spiritual: Brings wisdom; grounding and protective
Magical: Protection during travel; good luck; love; healing
Note: Do not use in direct-method gem elixirs as this stone contains copper

Stone: Unakite
Usual Colour: Mottled pink and green
Physical: Helps the reproductive system; assists in weight gain; improves strength
Emotional: Balances the emotions
Mental: Increases consciousness
Spiritual: For use in rebirthing; for self growth; spiritual freedom
Magical: For balance; healing the past; reconciliation

References and Resources

Further Reading

Love is in The Earth, Melody, Earth-Love Publishing House, Colorado 1995.
Love is in The Earth Kaleidoscopic Pictorial Supplement A, Melody, Earth-Love Publishing House, Colorado 1997.
Love is in The Earth Kaleidoscopic Pictorial Supplement Z, Melody, Earth-Love Publishing House, Colorado 1999.
The Crystal Bible, Judy Hall, Godsfield Press, Alresford 2003.
Crystals and Crystal Healing, Simon Lilly, Anness Publishing Ltd, London 1998.
Healing With Crystals and Chakra Energies, Sue and Simon Lilly, Anness Publishing Ltd, London 2003.
Crystal Power, Crystal Healing, Michael Gienger, Cassell plc, London 1998.
Crystal Wisdom, Andy Baggott and Morningstar, Piatkus, London 1999.
The Colour of Life, Judith Collins, Geddes & Grosset, Scotland 2005.

Crystals

Kernowcraft – a good section of reasonable priced crystals, tumble polished stones and beads. www.kernowcraft.com
Kacha Stones – ethically sourced crystals. www.kacha-stones.co.uk

Crystal Healing Courses

The Association of Melody Crystal Healing Instructors (TAOMCHI) www.taomchi.com
The International Association of Crystal Healing Therapists (IACHT) www.iacht.co.uk

FREE DETAILED CATALOGUE

Capall Bann is owned and run by people actively involved in many of the areas in which we publish. A detailed illustrated catalogue is available on request, SAE or International Postal Coupon appreciated. **Titles can be ordered direct from Capall Bann,** by post (cheque or PO with order), via our web site **www.capallbann.co.uk** using credit/debit card or Paypal, or from good bookshops and specialist outlets.

Angels and Goddesses - Celtic Christianity & Paganism, M. Howard
The Art of Conversation With the Genius Loci, Barry Patterson
Auguries and Omens - The Magical Lore of Birds, Yvonne Aburrow
Asyniur - Women's Mysteries in the Northern Tradition, S McGrath
Beginnings - Geomancy, Builder's Rites & Electional Astrology, Nigel Pennick
Between Earth and Sky, Julia Day
The Book of Seidr, Runic John
Caer Sidhe - Celtic Astrology and Astronomy, Michael Bayley
Call of the Horned Piper, Nigel Jackson
Carnival of the Animals, Gregor Lamb
Cat's Company, Ann Walker
Celebrating Nature, Gordon MacLellan
Celtic Faery Shamanism, Catrin James
Celtic Lore & Druidic Ritual, Rhiannon Ryall
Company of Heaven, Jan McDonald
Compleat Vampyre - The Vampyre Shaman, Nigel Jackson
Cottage Witchcraft, Jan McDonald
Crystal Clear - A Guide to Quartz Crystal, Jennifer Dent
Crystal Doorways, Simon & Sue Lilly
Crossing the Borderlines - Guising, Masking & Ritual Animal Disguise, Nigel Pennick
Dragons of the West, Nigel Pennick
Dreamtime by Linda Louisa Dell
Earth Dance - A Year of Pagan Rituals, Jan Brodie
Earth Harmony - Places of Power, Holiness & Healing, Nigel Pennick
Earth Magic, Margaret McArthur
Egyptian Animals - Guardians & Gateways of the Gods, Akkadia Ford
Eildon Tree (The) Romany Language & Lore, Michael Hoadley
Enchanted Forest - The Magical Lore of Trees, Yvonne Aburrow
Everything You Always Wanted To Know About Your Body, But So Far
    Nobody's Been Able To Tell You, Chris Thomas & D Baker
Experiencing the Green Man, Rob Hardy & Teresa Moorey
Fairies in the Irish Tradition, Molly Gowen

Familiars - Animal Powers of Britain, Anna Franklin
Flower Wisdom, Katherine Kear
Handbook For Pagan Healers, Liz Joan
Handbook of Fairies, Ronan Coghlan
Healing Book, The, Chris Thomas and Diane Baker
Healing Homes, Jennifer Dent
Healing Journeys, Paul Williamson
Healing Stones, Sue Philips
Heathen Paths - Viking and Anglo Saxon Beliefs by Pete Jennings
Herb Craft - Shamanic & Ritual Use of Herbs, Lavender & Franklin
In Search of Herne the Hunter, Eric Fitch
In Search of the Green Man, Peter Hill
In Search of Pagan Gods, Teresa Moorey
Legend of Robin Hood, The, Richard Rutherford-Moore
Lore of the Sacred Horse, Marion Davies
Lost Lands & Sunken Cities (2nd ed.), Nigel Pennick
Lyblác, Anglo Saxon Witchcraft by Wulfeage
The Magic and Mystery of Trees, Teresa Moorey
Magic For the Next 1,000 Years, Jack Gale
Magical Guardians - Exploring the Spirit and Nature of Trees, Philip Heselton
Magical History of the Horse, Janet Farrar & Virginia Russell
Magical Lore of Animals, Yvonne Aburrow
Magical Lore of Cats, Marion Davies
Magical Lore of Herbs, Marion Davies
The Magical Properties of Plants - and How to Find Them by Tylluan Penry
Masks of Misrule - Horned God & His Cult in Europe, Nigel Jackson
Mirrors of Magic - Evoking the Spirit of the Dewponds, P Heselton
The Moon and You, Teresa Moorey
Moon Mysteries, Jan Brodie
Mysteries of the Runes, Michael Howard
Mystic Life of Animals, Ann Walker
Pagan Feasts - Seasonal Food for the 8 Festivals, Franklin & Phillips
Paganism For Teens, Jess Wynne
Patchwork of Magic - Living in a Pagan World, Julia Day
Pathworking - A Practical Book of Guided Meditations, Pete Jennings
Personal Power, Anna Franklin
Pickingill Papers - The Origins of Gardnerian Wicca, Bill Liddell
Pillars of Tubal Cain, Nigel Jackson
Planet Earth - The Universe's Experiment, Chris Thomas
Practical Divining, Richard Foord
Practical Meditation, Steve Hounsome
Psychic Self Defence - Real Solutions, Jan Brodie
Romany Tapestry, Michael Houghton
Sacred Animals, Gordon MacLellan
Sacred Celtic Animals, Marion Davies, Ill. Simon Rouse
Sacred Dorset - On the Path of the Dragon, Peter Knight

Sacred Grove - The Mysteries of the Forest, Yvonne Aburrow
Sacred Geometry, Nigel Pennick
Sacred Ring - Pagan Origins of British Folk Festivals, M. Howard
Seasonal Magic - Diary of a Village Witch, Paddy Slade
Secret Places of the Goddess, Philip Heselton
Secret Signs & Sigils, Nigel Pennick
The Secrets of East Anglian Magic, Nigel Pennick
A Seeker's Guide To Past Lives, Paul Williamson
A Seer's Guide To Crystal Divination, Gale Halloran
Self Enlightenment, Mayan O'Brien
Spirits of the Earth series, Jaq D Hawkins
Talking to the Earth, Gordon MacLellan
Talking With Nature, Julie Hood
The Other Kingdoms Speak, Helena Hawley
Transformation of Housework, Ben Bushill
Treading the Mill - Practical CraftWorking in Modern Trad Witchcraft by Nigel Pearson
Tree: Essence of Healing, Simon & Sue Lilly
Tree: Essence, Spirit & Teacher, Simon & Sue Lilly
Tree Seer, Simon & Sue Lilly
Understanding Chaos Magic, Jaq D Hawkins
Understanding Second Sight, Dilys Gater
Understanding Spirit Guides, Dilys Gater
Understanding Star Children, Dilys Gater
The Urban Shaman, Dilys Gater
Walking the Tides - Seasonal Rhythms and Traditional Lore, Nigel Pearson
West Country Wicca, Rhiannon Ryall
What's Your Poison? vol 1, Tina Tarrant
Wheel of the Year, Teresa Moorey & Jane Brideson
Wildwitch - The Craft of the Natural Psychic, Poppy Palin
Wildwood King , Philip Kane
A Wisewoman's Book of Tea Leaf Reading, Pat Barki
The Witch's Kitchen, Val Thomas
Witchcraft Myth Magic Mystery and... Not Forgetting Fairies, Ralph Harvey
Wondrous Land - The Faery Faith of Ireland by Dr Kay Mullin
Working With Crystals, Shirley o'Donoghue
The Zodiac Experience, Patricia Crowther

FREE detailed catalogue

Contact: Capall Bann Publishing, Auton Farm,
Milverton, Somerset, TA4 1NE
www.capallbann.co.uk